THE PANIZ

19

THE PANIZZI LECTURES
1990

Erasmus, Colet and More:
The early Tudor Humanists
and their Books

J. B. TRAPP

THE BRITISH LIBRARY

For
Elayne

© 1991 J. B. Trapp

First published 1991 by
The British Library
Great Russell Street
London WC1B 3DG

British Library Cataloguing
in Publication Data is
available from The British Library

ISBN 0 7123 0256 5

Designed by John Mitchell
Typeset in Linotron Bembo
by Bexhill Phototypesetters, Bexhill-on-Sea
Printed in England by
Henry Ling, Dorchester

Contents

Preface

The sixth Panizzi Lectures in Bibliography are less concerned than their predecessors with bibliography in the strict sense. Put together as I could rather than entirely as I would, they lay emphasis on the content as well as on the physical make-up and the ownership of the works with which they deal. My hope is that something has been said that is interesting rather than comprehensive about that curious hybrid, early Tudor humanism, and its practitioners.

Janet Backhouse, Nicolas Barker, Ronald Browne, Martin Davies, Ian Doyle, Lotte Hellinga, Jill Kraye, Elizabeth McGrath and Andrew Prescott have kindly attended to some of my deficiencies in preparing the lectures for publication and I am grateful to them. They are not responsible for those that remain.

I have to thank the Committee of the Panizzi Foundation for their invitation, and the generous benefactress by whom the annual series are maintained.

J. B. TRAPP
February 1991

ACKNOWLEDGEMENTS

Grateful acknowledgement is made to the following for permission to reproduce objects in their charge: The Warden and Fellows of All Souls College, Oxford; The Bodleian Library, Oxford; The British Library Board; The Syndics of Cambridge University Library; Corpus Christi College, Cambridge; The President and Fellows of Corpus Christi College, Oxford; The Founders Society, Detroit Institute of Arts; The Folger Shakespeare Library, Washington D.C.; The Frick Collection, New York; The Provost and Scholars of King's College, Cambridge; Lambeth Palace Library; the Centrale Bibliotheek, Katholieke Universiteit Leuven; The Worshipful Company of Mercers; Her Majesty the Queen; The Marquess of Salisbury; The Master and Fellows of University College, Oxford; The Dean and Chapter of Wells; York Minster Library.

Photographic credits: The Bodleian Library, Oxford: 7, 9, 37; The British Library: 1–2, 6, 11, 14, 17, 23–24, 28–29, 31–34, 36, 38–41, 43, 48, 50–51; Cambridge University Library: 30, 42; Courtauld Institute of Art: 22, 35; Detroit Institute of Arts: 25; The Frick Collection: 19; The Surveyor of the Queen's Pictures: 21; Thomas Photos, Oxford: 3; The Warburg Institute: 5, 10, 13, 15, 18, 20, 26–27, 46–47, 49, 52–53; York Minster Library: 12.

Before Erasmus

Sir Anthony Panizzi would not, I am sure, have been displeased to find Sir Frederic Madden's Department of Manuscripts figuring large in a lecture series that bears his name. Whether Madden would have been equally happy to be associated with his rival, even at such a remove, is open to doubt. The plain fact is, however, that historians of the book must concern themselves with manuscripts as well as printed books, and use the evidence of one type of record to support that of the other. In other words, we all must be printed book people as well as manuscript people – or, if we cannot be both ourselves, we must seek support. As for me, I have needed the assistance of both sorts, generously given and here gratefully acknowledged.

The 'books' of my title, then, are both manuscripts and printed books, and they are often illustrated. They are the books that the early Tudor humanists – Desiderius Erasmus, John Colet and Thomas More above all – wrote, had written or printed for them, owned, read and used. In other words, I am writing about texts rather than books. 'Humanists' are humanists in the technical Renaissance sense, doubtful though it must remain whether any of the native Englishmen I shall deal with can lay claim to the title in that sense. The word 'humanist' originated in Italy – like so much else that has made Europe, usually for the best, what it is today. Specifically, it originated in late fifteeenth-century university patois, where it had come to be used of a teacher in the progressive educational movement known as the *studia humanitatis*. The *studia humanitatis* made up a programme of study elaborated on the basis of what Cicero had had to say about a liberal education. Typically, the programme comprised grammar, rhetoric, poetry and history, with – most frequently – moral philosophy. These were studied preeminently, not to say exclusively, in the best Latin and Greek classical authors, including the Fathers of the Church, since these were held to have possessed knowledge that was superior in quality and in quantity to what had been current in medieval intellectual culture and remained the contemporary norm. Moreover, they were held both to have lived and thought and to have written records of life and thought in a superior and exemplary way. For this reason, the poet and historian were considered close relations, necessary for the preservation of ancient lore and for persuasion to the ancient truths and virtues that they chronicled. Great men there may have been before Agamemnon – as Horace tells us – but they died unknown, unwept, because they had had no Homer to sing them. So the poet, who is also moral philosopher, the historian, the writer, the scholar, because they can recover the past, are necessary components of society along with men of action. What they write will be effective and lasting if it is couched in the classical languages.

All this Petrarch told his audience on the Capitol in Rome, during the ceremony he had engineered there in emulation – so he believed – of the ancient Roman custom of poetic laureation. To seal his title to the honour, he had had himself royally and orally examined in Naples on the *Aeneid*. Virgil was always his Latin verse hero. The oration that he made on the Roman Capitol, moreover, was based on the oration on the name and nature of poetry delivered by his great Latin prose hero. Cicero's *Pro Archia poeta* provided him with much of his material and gave him his approach. Petrarch's Coronation Oration also teems with quotation and extrapolation from the ancient poets. His Greek examples come at second hand, for he could not read them in the original: familiarity with that language was the prerogative of later generations of humanists. Petrarch's belief, which it suited his successors as poets laureate to continue, that poets had actually been crowned with wreaths of bay on the Capitol, by the Emperors of ancient Rome, was erroneous. This does not matter. A recurring theme in these lectures is that what is or was believed to be true is usually more sympathetic and interesting that what is or was true (as far as that can be established).[1]

Petrarch's enthusiastic adumbration of what it was necessary to study and how it should be studied developed, in the generations that followed him, and largely through his disciples, into the educational curriculum I have already briefly characterized. Just how this happened, and just how humanist philology came to be applied also to the most sacred and inviolable of texts, the New Testament, delivered and maintained under the inspiration of the Holy Ghost and so secure from corruption, is not my concern here. One needs to note in passing, however, the name of perhaps the greatest humanist of all, since it will recur. Lorenzo Valla towers among his fifteenth-century contemporaries and exerts a vastly broad and general influence. It is true that, in the development of classical scholarship Poliziano, from later in the century, is the greater name. One of the beliefs on which these lectures rest, however, is that Britain – in my period at least – is a provincial place, in so far as she produced no classical scholar equal to the highest Italian professional standards until the birth of Richard Bentley in the late seventeenth century. No important edition of a major classical author and hardly, even, of a minor one was made by an Englishman, on English soil, or printed in England until the great Eton Chrysostom of 1610–12. This Greek text is symptomatic also of the way in which English printing seems to leap from ugliness and ineptitude in the sixteenth century to mastery in the seventeenth. Fine scholars there were, Isaac Casaubon

---

1 See E. H. Wilkins, *The Making of the Canzoniere and other Petrarchan Studies*, Rome 1951, pp.9ff.; and J. B. Trapp, *Essays on the Renaissance and the classical Tradition*, Aldershot 1990, ii, pp.93–130; iii, pp.227–55.

among them, who spent time in Britain in the later sixteenth century; and, among Britons, there was always George Buchanan, greatest of pedagogues, much of whose time was spent in France. In general, however, with the striking exceptions of the Dutchman Desiderius Erasmus and the Spaniard Juan Luis Vives in the first quarter of the sixteenth century, these either stayed very briefly or did not arrive until the very end of the century. None of the mid-fifteenth-century worthies whom I shall briefly mention in a moment can be thought of in contemporary Italian company. Of the generation with whom I shall be particularly concerned only Thomas Linacre attained the requisite standard in Greek and Latin learning.[2] Linacre, with his assistance in the Aldine Aristotle and his new Latin translations of Galen, in particular, which soon became standard, is also Britain's only early representative – and a very considerable one – of the humanism that concerns itself with the literature that offers the more practical benefits of science and technology: medicine, warfare and architecture, for example, Galen, Vegetius, Frontinus and Vitruvius. Linacre's English fellow-students in Florence, William Grocyn and William Latimer, having left us next to nothing by which to form an estimate, can hardly lay claim to the status. Nor can the schoolmaster generation of the time of which I shall be speaking, either those with European experience – even such as William Lily – or without, such as Stanbridge, Whittinton, Horman of Eton, Rightwise of St Paul's. Nor, to go later, Roger Ascham, Sir John Cheke and the rest. Not to labour the point too much, it is worth observing that the name of Poliziano occurs seldom in English library catalogues during the Renaissance. There are some notable exceptions, in particular an anonymous and highly interesting list of the 1550s – in which Cheke is twice mentioned as a borrower – now part of Additional MS 40676 in the British Library.

Much of Poliziano's influence was *viva voce* rather than exerted through print. The situation with Valla was entirely

2 *Linacre Studies: Essays on the Life and Work of T. Linacre*, ed. F. Maddison, M. Pelling and C. Webster, Oxford 1977.

different. His *De elegantiis linguae latinae*, that great exemplar of the humanist *methodice* notebook, was enormously popular from the moment of its first printing in 1471, and enormously accessible. Even in English libraries and booksellers' lists it is frequently met with. For Erasmus, it was the most important of books: he made an epitome of it, and he urged Cornelis Gerard to get to know it as well as he knew his own fingers and toes.[3] Valla, too, has a claim in terms of the bold stroke that lays open a whole broad area not merely of letters but of experience, changing orientation irrevocably. 'Is any authority superior to reason?' was his famous question. His *Annotationes in Novum Testamentum* exemplified this attitude in its application of philological principle and reasoned philological method to that most sacrosanct of texts, the Vulgate, comparing its wording and its sense with that of its original Greek. His treatise on the Donation of Constantine used the same humanist instruments on a much later document, almost equally hallowed by Church tradition. Ulrich von Hutten had already introduced it into the Reformation debate before it was translated into English and issued as 'the declamation of L. Valla, against the forged donation' in 1534.[4]

Erasmus's admiration for Valla's philological example was enormous; in early days he truculently styled himself Valla's avenger and defender in scholarship.[5] Valla's status as Erasmian hero was confirmed by the discovery, in the abbey of Parc near Louvain during 1504, of a manuscript of the *Annotationes in Novum Testamentum*, which Erasmus had printed, for the first time, at Paris in 1505. That first edition was, as it happens, dedicated to an Englishman, Christopher Fisher, protonotary apostolic, in return for hospitality. If Valla had wrought the great change with his *Elegantiae*, it was Erasmus who played an

---

3 Letter 29; ?1489; *Opus epistolarum D. Erasmi Roterodami*, i, ed. P. S. Allen, Oxford 1906, p.120 [hereafter: Allen]; *Correspondence of Erasmus*, i, trans. R. A. B. Mynors and D. F. S. Thomson, annotated W. K. Ferguson, Toronto 1974, p.54 [hereafter: *Correspondence*].
4 G. R. Elton, *Policy and Police: The Enforcement of the Reformation in the Age of Thomas Cromwell*, Cambridge 1972, pp.174, 186,n.2.
5 Letter to Cornelis Gerard, cit. n.3 above.

almost equal part as middleman by putting the *Annotationes* into printed circulation. The *Annotationes* changed the face of learning, but they also changed the face of orthodox Western Christianity, in ways which it took time for Western Christianity to fathom, despite the clear message of the preface that Erasmus wrote for his edition, about March 1505.[6] There could hardly be a better illustration of how intellectual-spiritual change, initiated in what it is now fashionable to call an élite, enlarges itself and its influence as it goes until it comes to occupy all areas of sentience. The *Annotationes*, incidentally, figure in that interesting library list to which I have referred, along with other unidentified works by Valla.

Valla's *Annotationes* were not less important for taking time about their effect. More than half a century elapsed between their composition and their first printing and – as we shall see – the figure now known as ps.-Dionysius the Areopagite took some two centuries to die, in his capacity as the convert and disciple of St Paul, at least, after Valla had given him the death-blow in a brief note on Acts 17.34. Who knows how long Valla would have lain in manuscript, monastically cobwebbed in the classic humanist style, had Erasmus not chanced upon him in Louvain – ironically enough, in view of his later encounters with the Faculty of Theology there – at a particular moment in his progress, when he had already embarked full strength, full sail on sacred letters, and at the time of the publication of the *Enchiridion militis Christiani*, that first summing up of the guiding principles of his – and others' - religious life. His weapons for spiritual battle were already bright in his hands.

There is a parallel, admittedly at a higher level, between what Erasmus did for Valla and what he did for his English friends. The service he did Valla in ensuring his circulation in a mode going far deeper than the verbal, in a sense making Valla's reputation for him in Northern Europe, is akin to what he did for Thomas More and John Colet in particular among those who had befriended and aided him in England: two remarkable portrait letters, one of them an obituary, as well as many others

6 Letter 182; Allen, i, pp.406–12; *Correspondence*, ii, pp.89–97.

exchanged with one or other of them, with innumerable other commendations in letters and elsewhere, published in one or other of Erasmus's collections, made these names sound in Europe as they would never otherwise have done. Consider, too, the preface to the *Encomium Moriae*, where More is first termed 'a man for all seasons', the controversy with Maarten van Dorp over the *Folly* and the New Testament, and the arrangements shared by Erasmus and Pieter Gillis for the publication of *Utopia* at Louvain in 1516, and the part of Erasmus in the second printing, at Paris in 1517, not to speak of the third and fourth in Basel, by Froben, early and late in 1518.[7] Compared with the momentous consequences of the *Annotationes*, these are less in scale. They are nevertheless of the first importance for early Tudor humanism. There is a strong sense, indeed, in which that phenomenon was the creation of Erasmus. Certainly it was a far different thing after Erasmus's advent than it had been before.

These digressive introductory reflexions – necessary, I believe, to understand certain of the activities of the Englishmen I shall be concerned with in these lectures – have taken me backwards, so to speak, through my title. The consideration of Petrarch and Valla is intended as background to its penultimate element, the humanists, evangelical humanists at that, and as a hint at the importance of Greek studies, and a more modest hint at Hebrew. They have brought me somewhat ahead of myself. A little still needs to be said about the fourteenth- and fifteenth-century background to the humanism, pure and applied, of the reigns of Henry VII and Henry VIII. A formidable amount of work remains to be done before we can have any real sort of understanding of the after-life of antiquity in English culture during those, or any other centuries.[8] Perhaps the single most

7 Useful brief summaries in the entries for Colet and More in *Contemporaries of Erasmus: A biographical Register of the Renaissance and Reformation*, ed. P. G. Bietenholz and T. B. Deutscher, Toronto, i, 1985, pp.324–8 (Colet); ii, 1986, pp.451–59 (More family); and see further below.

8 For fourteenth-century England, Beryl Smalley, *English Friars and Antiquity in the early Fourteenth Century*, Oxford 1960, is exemplary and points the way; Roberto Weiss, *Humanism in England during the Fifteenth Century*, 3rd. edition,

important task is a full and accurate assessment of the rôle of French civilization as mediator of the Italian neo-classical programme and its products, which continues far beyond the time with which I am dealing. This is not to deny the primacy of Italy's share in framing the new blueprint for intellectual life, nor Italy's continuing presence. Poggio Bracciolini, for example, was secretary to Cardinal Beaufort from 1418 to 1422, though he returned home notoriously dissatisfied with the lean harvest of classical texts he had gathered. The papal collectors, Piero del Monte for instance, in England from 1435 to 1440, were influential among those - chiefly in the circle of Humfrey Duke of Gloucester - receptive to humanist studies. Humfrey did his best by inviting Leonardo Bruni Aretino to England – but, on Bruni's declining the invitation, he was able to obtain for his 'poet and orator' no-one better than Tito Livio Frulovisi, the pupil – probably – of Guarino of Verona.[9] Frulovisi was succeeded by a humanist of similar make, Antonio Beccaria, the pupil of Vittorino da Feltre. Humfrey's patronage of Bruni, his admiration for Bruni's translation of Aristotle's *Nicomachean Ethics*, and his request for a new version of the *Politics* show him, however, as one who knew what quality was and who hoped to obtain it. It is to be remembered also that Pier Candido Decembrio's translation of Plato's *Republic* was dedicated to Humfrey. We remember, too, Humfrey's activities as collector and donor of books.[10]

Oxford 1967, is invaluable as a guide, but treats humanism in its own terms and from an exclusively Italian point of view. A highly satisfactory brief survey is Denys Hay, 'England and the Humanities in the Fifteenth Century', *Itinerarium Italicum*, ed. H. A. Oberman and T. A. Brady Jr., Leiden 1975, pp.307–67; and see the brief account by J. B. Trapp in *Artemis Lexikon des Mittelalters*, iii, Munich 1989, cols. 199–201.

9 *Opera hactenus inedita T. Livii de Frulovisiis de Ferrara*, ed. C. W. Previté Orton, Cambridge 1932; R. Weiss, 'Humphrey Duke of Gloucester and Tito Livio Frulovisi', *Fritz Saxl 1890–1948: A Volume of memorial Essays from his Friends in England*, ed. D. J. Gordon, London 1957, pp.218–27.

10 For Humfrey, see now A. Sammut, *Unfredo duca di Gloucester e gli umanisti italiani*, Padua 1980; A. C. de la Mare, *Duke Humfrey's Library and the Divinity School*, catalogue of the exhibition in the Bodleian Library, Oxford 1988,

In addition to princely collectors and patrons such as Humfrey, there were the magnates and the prelates. John Tiptoft, Earl of Worcester, for example, was the most Italianate of English nobles, scholar and patron of scholars, with a fine collection of texts. William Gray, later Bishop of Ely (d. 1478), had a taste for theology tempered by a personal association with Guarino of Verona, and commissioned or bought manuscripts from scribes and book-providers such as T. Werken and Vespasiano da Bisticci. Andrew Holes, too, was Vespasiano's client and earned a biography from Vespasiano. Werken, indeed, found it worth-while to follow Gray from Cologne to Italy in the expectation of commissions, and Vespasiano, having supplied Gray with still more books in the fashionable style, judged him to deserve a biography in the *Vite degli uomini illustri*. Gray patronized other scribes such as Antonio Mario and Gherardo del Ciriagio and scholars such as Niccolò Perotti; and he was the acquaintance of the antiquary Giovanni Marcanova, of Cardinal Bessarion and of Poggio Bracciolini himself. Somewhat down the social scale are others such as Robert Flemmyng, scholar and diplomat, with a command of Greek and a substantial library; and – also approaching the pattern of the Italian professional humanist – the short-lived John Free, whose talents secured him respect even from Italian scholars, the most gifted of any generation before that of Grocyn and Linacre. So one could continue, naming individuals who, having experienced the Italian programme of the *studia humanitatis* brought it back, in one degree or another, to their native country. An index of acclimatization is the clear ability to write the Italian hand on the part of English scribes in the mid-fifteenth century.[11]

Some sort of presence of Italian humanists and humanism is, then, continuous in England from the early fifteenth century. As often as not, however, the French presence is stronger and

with continuations in *Bodleian Library Record*, xiii, 1988 and subsequent volumes.
11 See especially, A. C. de la Mare, 'Humanistic Hands in England', *Manuscripts at Oxford. An Exhibition in Memory of R. W. Hunt*, ed. A. C. de la Mare and B. C. Barker-Benfield, Oxford 1980, pp.93–101.

it is through France that a great many Latin works, classical, medieval or Renaissance, as well as the writings of Italian authors, find their way into English culture. This is already clear in Chaucer – for instance in such a work as the *Clerk's Tale*, where a French adaptation of Boccaccio's original Italian and probably of Petrarch's Latin version was the immediate source. Particularly about the time of the deposition of Henry VI, however, and the reign of Edward IV, that is to say during the 1460s and 1470s, the Netherlands add a renewed and vigorous force to the cultural quantum. It is not that influences of this sort and from this quarter had hitherto been lacking, especially in the eastern areas of England. It is that certain aspects of Netherlandish achievement in the arts of the book such as writing, illuminating and printing, become a norm for English commission and emulation. In scholarship, too, the impetus is great; and that will bring me to Erasmus. In this sense, at least, the Netherlands, with Paris intervening, are the decisive force in early Tudor humanism.

The royal library assembled by Edward IV in emulation of his host at Bruges, Louis de Gruthuyse, reflects a Burgundian-Netherlandish taste that is also reflected in many of the books that William Caxton was beginning to print for and in England from 1475. More than thirty volumes in the British Library can with certainty or with fair probability be associated with Edward. Some of the most famous among them – Royal MS 16 F.II, for example – having been begun for Edward, were later made over for Henry VII (Figs. 1–2). This has occasioned some confusion.[12] Henry – or perhaps it was his buyers – seems to have been at least as interested in printed books as in manuscripts, and by and large in French printed books, particularly those from Paris and the publisher Antoine Vérard.[13]

12 The matter has been admirably sorted out by Janet M. Backhouse, 'Founders of the Royal Library: Edward IV and Henry VII as Collectors of illuminated Manuscripts', *England in the Fifteenth Century: Proceedings of the Harlaxton Symposium for 1986*, ed. D. Williams, Woodbridge 1987, pp.23–41.
13 See, for example, T. A. Birrell, *English Monarchs and their Books: From Henry VII to Charles II. Panizzi Lectures 1986*, London 1987, pp.5–7; Eleanor P. Spencer, 'Antoine Vérard's illuminated Vellum Incunables', *Manuscripts in*

Es nouuelles Dalbion
Sil vous en plaist escouter
Mon frere & mon compaignio
Sachiez qua mon retorner
Ay este sera sa mer
Be ceu a Joyeuse chiere

1 British Library, Royal MS 16 F.II, fol. 73.

2 British Library, Royal MS 16 F.II, fol. 1.

My concern is only incidentally with royal taste, however. I shall from time to time touch on royal patronage, but I am preoccupied rather with what might be called sub-magnate, clerical, humanist and sub-humanist matters. I want to begin by re-examining the career, the taste, the reading of an influential cleric, royal servant and politician of the earlier Tudor period.[14] Christopher Urswick was a lawyer as well as an ecclesiastic; he had experience of Italian travel and he had contact, it seems, with Italian humanists; he had been in France; and he may well have crossed from there to Milford Haven with Henry VII, whose almoner and ambassador he was to be. His part in settling the Tudors on the throne cannot have been inconsiderable. He has a further claim on our attention as one of the circle of patrons assembled for himself by Erasmus in England.

In certain respects Urswick's life and career are parallel to those of Richard Fox (Fig.3), though Fox rose higher in office both in church and in state, and Fox is much the better known, especially for his 'beehive', Corpus Christi College Oxford, which he founded in 1517, about the time he vacated his state functions in favour of Thomas Wolsey.[15]

Neither Fox nor Urswick has left us much on which to base a judgment of their literary or humanist accomplishments. Both are more remarkable for what they caused others to do or to write. Urswick was born, of relatively humble parents it seems, perhaps in 1448. Educated at Cambridge, he soon became head of a college there; he was Dean successively of York and Windsor, registrar of the chivalric order of the Garter, confessor both to Henry and to his mother, the Lady Margaret. Moreover, he may well have been one of Thomas More's chief *viva voce*

the *Fifty Years after the Invention of Printing*, ed. J. B. Trapp, London 1983, pp.62–5; and Mary Beth Winn, 'Antoine Vérard's Presentation Manuscripts and printed Books', ibid., pp.66–74.

14 J. B. Trapp, 'Christopher Urswick and his Books: The Reading of Henry VII's Almoner', *Renaissance Studies*, i, 1987, pp.48–70; repr. id., *Essays on the Renaissance and the classical Tradition*, Aldershot 1990, xv, pp.48–70.

15 See the summary account in *Contemporaries of Erasmus*, ii, Toronto 1986, pp.46–9.

CLARVS WINTONIÆ PRÆSVL COGNOMINE FOXVS,
QVI PIVS HOC OLIM NOBILE STRVXIT OPVS
TALIS ERAT FORMA TALIS DVA VIXIT AMICTV
QVALEM SPECTANTI PICTA TABELIA REFERT.

HANC REPVRGATAM TABELLAM RESTITVIT IOHES HOOKER GENEROSVS
EXONIENSIS 1579

3 Johannes Corvus, Portrait of Bishop Fox. Oxford, Corpus Christi
College.

14

informants for his *History of Richard III* and therefore influential in reinforcing the Tudor idea of Richard as a monster. Though Urswick goes into affluent semi-retirement at about the time of Erasmus's second visit to England in 1505, or a little before, he remains sufficiently influential – or perhaps merely retains sufficient potential as a source of patronage – for Erasmus to send him both his *Novum Instrumentum* and his edition of St Jerome in 1516.[16] Our best source for a knowledge of Urswick is the books which survive from his library and the manuscripts he commissioned, almost all of them annotated, some copiously.

For my purposes, Urswick is an excellent example of the transitional figure of the age just before the London humanists, as they had best be called, rather than the Oxford Reformers – Grocyn, William Lily, Colet, More, Thomas Linacre – made their brief appearance on the European stage, on more or less equal terms with their European counterparts. A substantial presence up to the 1490s, to the time of Erasmus's first visit to England in 1499, let us say, he then begins to fade into the background. At fifty or so – like Thomas More thirty years later, at a similar age though for different reasons – he was perhaps thinking of himself as an old man, and growing a little weary of his rôle in the world. He assumes the position of elder statesman, yielding place to younger men without waiting to be washed out by the new wave under the young Henry VIII. My concern with him is because his formation belongs to the period before Erasmus visited England and, more importantly, because of the way that formation was applied to the commissioning of manuscripts. It is not easy to know where he bought his printed books, with one exception. The manuscripts he commissioned, on the other hand, all belong to the time from about 1503 to 1518. All were written for him by a single scribe, Pieter Meghen, the one-eyed Brabantine.[17]

16 Erasmus, Letters 451–2, 474; Allen, ii, pp.317–8,353–4; *Correspondence*, iv, pp.37–39, 90–93.
17 See *Contemporaries of Erasmus*, ii, 1986, pp.420–22; and J. B. Trapp, *Essays on the Renaissance and the classical Tradition*, Aldershot 1990, xiv, pp.1–3, figs. 1–16.

4 Wells Cathedral Library, MS Book 5, fol. 1.

The quality of these manuscripts is variable. In 1514, Urswick commissioned Meghen to write and to have decorated in the fashionable Ghent-Bruges style, a handsome Psalter to be presented to Hayles Abbey in memory of Sir John Huddleston; it bears prominently in its decoration the arms and motto – *Misericordia* – of Urswick as well as the badges of Henry VIII and Katherine of Aragon (Fig.4). Three years later Meghen completed, to Urswick's order and also for presentation to Hayles in memory of Huddleston, a Latin Chrysostom on St Matthew, copied – as was Meghen's almost invariable habit – from a printed edition.[18] Meghen used George of Trebizond's translation, and the codex again bears Urswick's arms and motto in its less accomplished Ghent-Bruges style decoration. Chrysostom was a favourite in forward-looking circles of the time. Grocyn had a Greek text of his sermons on Matthew written by one of the Greek scribes who, by the end of the fifteenth century, were living and working in England.[19]

The classical authors from Urswick's library are disappointing in both quantity and quality. His manuscript of Cicero *De officiis* and *Paradoxa* is a provincial performance of 1503. Now in Rouen, it is Meghen's first extant dated manuscript and the only real evidence of Urswick's involvement with the pagan moralists. Dedicated to Henry Daubeney, son of Giles, first Baron Daubeney, it seems to have been reclaimed at Giles's death in 1508 and given in 1509 to André Bouhier, abbot of Fécamp. No annotations betray its specific attractions for Urswick, though a prefatory letter underlines the value of the *De officiis* as the classic justification of the active humanist life, and its value as a guide to conduct. Of other classical authors, he owned a printed Statius, in the edition of Venice 1490; and a printed Quintus Curtius Rufus, in the edition of Venice 1494. The Statius is not annotated, but there are many notes of a lexical and factual nature in the Quintus Curtius, as well as a good deal of noting

---

18 On manuscripts copied from printed books, see M. D. Reeve in *Manuscripts in the Fifty Years after the Invention of Printing*, ed. J. B. Trapp, London 1983, pp.12–20.
19 Corpus Christi College, Oxford, MS. 23.

of examples and *sententiae* – Darius's mildness and tractability, the opulence of his court, his death; Alexander's continence and clemency and his character in general.

Four extant works only from Urswick's library can count as Italian humanist. Two are in manuscript and bound together; two are printed books. The manuscripts are Aeneas Sylvius Piccolomini, *Historia Bohemica* and Leonardo Bruni Aretino's re-working of Polybius *On the First Punic War*; the printed books are Marco Antonio Sabellico, *Res Venetae* (Venice 1487) and Platina, *Vitae pontificum* with the *De bono* and other works (Venice 1504). Urswick gave the Platina to the Dominicans of Lancaster, along with the three volumes of St Antoninus, *Opus historiale* in the edition of Basel 1491. Neither the Antoninus nor the Sabellico is annotated, so that we can only guess at Urswick's interest in them as storehouses of salutary examples. The manuscript duo, Aeneas Sylvius and Bruni, are more promising. There is no doubt that they are another case of printed books copied in manuscript, again by Pieter Meghen, the Aeneas Sylvius perhaps from the Rome printing of 1475 and the Bruni of 1490. A letter prefixed to the manuscript, from John Colet in Rome, dated 1 April 1493, apologizes for sending a printed version rather than the manuscript that Urswick had ordered before leaving Rome – and he exculpates himself by remarking that there is no need now of the pen, when the printing press stands available. What is important, he goes on – rather uncharacteristically, as we shall see, but in conventional humanist fashion – is both matter and manner. History is of the greatest utility for its *gravitas rerum* and most agreeable for its *varietas*. The work's most ancient style – still a term of approval – its *stilus vetustissimus*, the brevity and clarity of its narration, provide as much pleasure as its import. It is agreeable to think of Urswick reading his historians humanistically for stylistic pleasure as well as for soberer instructive purposes. One can think of worse humanist historians to choose than Aeneas Sylvius and Bruni to this end. In both these books Urswick's annotations are as usual partly catchwords, partly lexical notes – there is, alas, no sign of the stylistic appreciation recommended by Colet. In the Bruni, there is some noting of ancient example, but the annotation is relatively thin and peters out before the end. The annotations to Aeneas Sylvius are more copious and interesting. They begin with the Council of Constance and continue to the Council of Basel, showing much interest in Hus and in Jerome of Prague. The Continental progeny of Wiclif was a matter of concern to an English churchman and he clearly read these parts carefully, correcting the text concerning Peter Payne the Taborite and his accusation of Peter Partridge, the Chancellor of Lincoln, as having introduced him to Lollard doctrines. A good many *sententiae* of broad application are also marked, and the inexhaustible lust of the Emperor Sigismund's consort is twice noted. His chief thought, however, is for the Bohemian heresy, its English origin and its possible renewed or continuing danger to England.

Here, topicality seems to be the keynote, and moral reflexion; little or nothing is in evidence of any kind of rhetorical appreciation of the sort evidenced by his brief annotations – if they are in fact his – in a thirteenth- or fourteenth-century manuscript of Albertanus of Brescia's *De arte dicendi aut tacendi*. And there are no reader's marks in his manuscript of the French Mandeville.

Urswick's legal interests are apparent in his ownership of a handsome and handsomely bound, if somewhat assorted, set of the *Corpus iuris civilis*, in editions printed at Strasbourg between 1491 and 1500 and at Lyons in 1506 (Fig. 5). Certain sections, notably those concerning inheritances, are copiously annotated, perhaps indicating an interest of a legal-theory kind to add to Urswick's practical doings with wills under English ecclesiastical law, which were many.

Urswick's copies of Erasmus's edition of St Jerome, along with his copy of the *Novum Instrumentum*, having disappeared, we cannot know how they appeared to him. He may have been cynical enough to have understood that they had been sent in the hope that he would give Erasmus another horse, to replace the one presented much earlier and now past use; at all events there would have been some justice in that view. The original mount, so highly satisfactory, had been received in return for the dedication of Erasmus's Latin version of Lucian's *Gallus*, printed at Paris towards the end of 1506. How far Urswick

5 York Minster Library, Urswick's *Corpus iuris civilis*. Binding.

would have accepted the view of Lucian the scourge of those who abuse ecclesiastical privilege – as presented by Thomas More in his letter to Thomas Ruthall, prefixed to the Lucian of 1506 – is not recoverable.[20] Nevertheless, Urwick may be thought to be content with an association with the *avant garde* pious circle in which Erasmus was moving, which he had indeed part created: Fox, Colet, More and the rest. There can be no doubt of his concern for the state and status of the church and the priesthood, at any rate: it was profound and sincere. His piety, less forward-looking and far less incandescent than Colet's, was perfectly conscious that inward conviction must both support and be supported by outward observance. He was open to influences of a proto-reforming kind from Erasmus and, as we shall see, from Savonarola.

On the other hand, Urswick's encounter with one of the basic texts of Christendom, as recorded in his copy of St Augustine's *De civitate Dei*, in the edition printed at Venice in 1475,[21] which is, rather grandly, a vellum copy, is not enlightening. He copiously annotates Book I, in which Augustine initiates his attack on the proposition that the sack of Rome by Alaric and his Goths in 410 was a judgment by the gods on a city that had abandoned their cult for the worship of Christ. He addresses such mighty questions as why 'the gracious mercies of God were extended unto such ungodly and ungrateful wretches as well as to his true servants; and why the afflictions of this siege fell upon the godly (in part) as well as on the reprobate', and how Christians ought to react to such a situation.[22] At I.25 he seems to lose interest until Book XI. The second chapter of this book is annotated by Urswick and later used elsewhere by him. It concerns itself succinctly but importantly with 'the knowledge of God, which none can attain but through the mediator

---

20 *Translations of Lucian*, ed. Craig R. Thompson, New Haven and London 1974, p.7 = Yale Edition, iii,1; *Correspondence of Sir Thomas More*, ed. Elizabeth Frances Rogers, Princeton 1947, p.13.
21 Now Corpus Christi College, Cambridge, MS. 346; M. R. James, *Descriptive Catalogue of the MSS in the Library of Corpus Christi College, Cambridge*, ii, Cambridge 1911, p.181.
22 I use the translation of John Healey (1610).

between God and man, the man Christ Jesus' – doctrine at once vital, central and conventional. How much of the Augustinian charge, the force and significance they derive from their context, whether immediate, remote or cumulative, is retained by such words as they pass through Urswick's mind to his pen and to the margins of his book is, however, next to impossible to gauge. A fairly constant interest in exemplary Roman history – Regulus, say, and the suicide of Cato – is discernible. And Urswick wrestles with an important Augustinian thesis concerning the justice, mercy and patience of God: 'If all sin were in the present punished, there should be nothing to do at the last judgment; and again, if no sin were here publicly punished, the divine providence would not be believed.'

This is, on the whole, a drab encounter with a great work. Urswick's dealings with the distinctly second-rate of a thousand years later are perhaps more revealing. His copy of Platina's *Works* of 1504 is now in the Bodleian. Its annotation is brief and sketchy in the *Lives of the Popes*, but full in the *De vero falsoque bono* which, despite its derivative and conventional character was, like others of Platina's moral works, highly popular and widely read.

From this I turn to a final group of nine or ten manuscripts – according to how they are counted – and perhaps a printed book from the press of Richard Pynson. Seven, or six and a half, of the manuscripts were certainly written by Pieter Meghen; one contains a letter from Urswick to Prior Thomas Goldstone of Canterbury on the present state of the Church. This manuscript, once – it turns out – part of the Cotton collection, is now Additional MS 15673 in the British Library (Fig.6).[23] Five of the manuscripts were written for Urswick between 1504 and 1518 or so; another was probably written for him, yet another possibly. All will help to fill out the picture I am attempting of the man and his interests. The common denominators are ecclesiological, theological and devotional.

Douce MS 110 in the Bodleian Library, containing the Cano-

23 I owe to Janet Backhouse my knowledge that this manuscript belonged to Cotton.

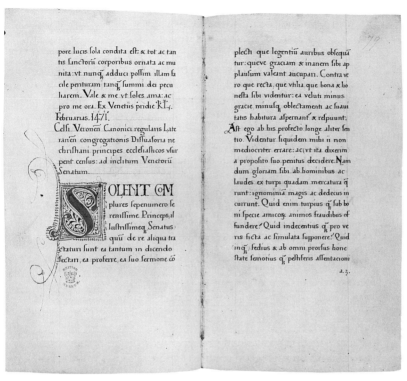

nical Epistles, Ecclesiastes, ps-Ambrose on the priesthood and extracts from St Augustine's *Soliloquies*, was completed for Urswick by Meghen on 28 November 1504 (or 1505) and possibly decorated in England. The ps-Ambrose text, though a favourite with Urswick, and more than once transcribed for him, is not annotated by him here or elsewhere. He worries away, on the other hand, at Ecclesiastes 8, and what the wise man is to do when he sins by omission or commission.

The ps-Ambrose text appears again in Rawlinson MS A.431 (Fig. 7) and in Barlow MS 14 in the Bodleian Library, both also

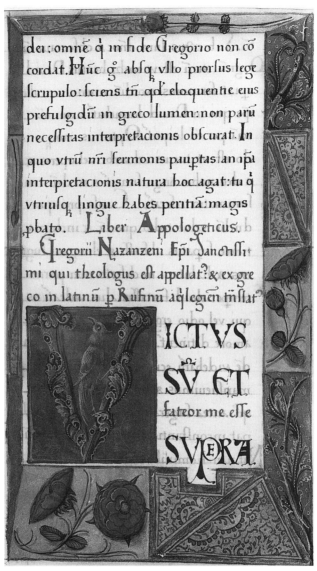

dei:omné q̃ in fide Gregorio non cõ
cordat. Huc g̃ abſq̃ vllo prorſus lege
ſcrupulo: ſciens tñ qd̃ eloquentie eius
prefulgidũ in greco lumen:non parũ
neceſſitas interpretacionis obſcurat. In
quo vtrũ nr̃i ſermonis pauptas an ipſi
interpretacionis natura hoc agat:tu q̃
vtriuſq̃ lingue habes peritiã:magis
pbato. Liber Appologeticus.
Gregorii Nazanzeni Epi Sanctiſſi
mi qui theologus eſt appellat? & ex gre
co in latinũ p Rufinũ a q̃ legitẽ tñſlat?

ICTVS
SV ET
fateor me eſſe
SVPRA

7 Oxford, Bodleian Library, Rawlinson MS A.431, fol.3r.

siliario usus meo & ipso non malo: ut
opinor: sin minus certe uel sedulo
dicta factaq que ad pietate perti
nent potius ignorans: malim doceri
qm docere. Optabile nanq est mihi *hoc il Gregorij*
percaroq ad ultima discere senectu *affectus*
te. Quoniaquide nulla etas ad per
discendu sufficere potest. Docere uero
alios affectare: & qui non sufficienter
instructus est res mihi uidet antiq | *Antiqu pronbii*
pronerby. In dolio discere arte figu
li. hoc est in periculo animaru docti
na discere pietatis. Quiq aut satis
stulti mihi uident aut temerarij.
Stulti pro eo si in tantu bruti sut *Stult q*
ut imperito se esse non sentiant: teme *t. temerarij? (o*
rarij si intelligant queda audent ta
men adire negotiu. Hebreox seni *Antiqua hebreoru*
ores tradunt qd fuerit talis queda *laudabilis obsuaco*
apud eos antiquitus laudabilis ob

8 Washington, D.C., Folger Shakespeare Library, MS V.α.84.

written by Meghen and again, perhaps, decorated in England. The Barlow MS, with its inferior imitation Ghent-Bruges border, contains another favourite text of Urswick's: Celso Maffei of Verona's *Dissuasoria ne christiani principes ecclesiasticos usurpent census*, together with his *Quaestio an aliqua respublica possit conducere Judeos ad fenerandum sine peccato*. This is the only appearance of the latter tract in an English context, to which at this time it could have had no relevance. The text dissuading secular rulers from interference with the church by its warning of the dire fate that befell the temerarious in this respect, from Antiochus to Heliodorus, and on to the Emperor Frederick II, the Carrara lords of Padua and Filippo Maria Strozzi, was, it seems, circulated by Urswick in manuscript among the influential; and he may well have been behind its sole English printing by Pynson in 1505. There was a clear relevance here to clutching laymen's habits in Henry VII's times.

A more personal concern seems to lie behind two manuscripts, one opulent and late, and the other early and much less elaborate. MS V.α.84 in the Folger Shakespeare Library, the less attractive of the pair, was written by Meghen at Urswick's instruction and charge in 1504 (Fig.8). It bears his arms and motto and its chief component is the Latin translation by Rufinus of St Gregory Nazianzenus's *Apologeticus*. This tract on personal holiness and the duties of religious men was clearly significant for Urswick: he had it transcribed three times.[24] It does not, however, appear in the most handsome of the manuscripts written for Urswick himself: University College, Oxford MS 40, which must on both textual and palaeographical grounds date from after 1517 (Fig.9). In it are two sermons by St John Chrysostom, one in the Latin of George of Trebizond and the other in that of Prior William Sellyng of Canterbury. It once contained two impeccably orthodox sermons by Martin Luther, though the leaves containing them have been cut out at some unidentifiable date. It contains St Augustine on the Lord's

---

24 In the Folger MS, and in two Bodleian MSS, Rawlinson A.431 and Barlow 14.

Homelia xiii dum Joannis Chrisostom
ex euangelii sancti Matthei cap. v. & vi.

VDISTIS
quia di
ctum est
antiquis:
Diliges
proximu
tuu:& odio
habebis in
imicu tuu
Ego aute
dico: Diligite inimicos ves tros:

Cce sextum mandatum legem
adimplens: minimu apud ho
mines odibiles, et inuicem odientes
qui inimicu odiri debere, improba
voce pronunciare non erubescunt.
Quod si iustum fuisset inimicos odire

9 Oxford, University College, MS 40, fol. 1.

27

10 Lambeth Palace Library, MS 3561, fols.67v–68.

Prayer, and it contains Girolamo Savonarola's *Meditations* on the 30th and the 50th Psalms.

Savonarola in England is a subject that needs much more attention than it has so far had. The *Meditations* in question were printed in Latin in both London and Paris in the first years of the sixteenth century; and later in both English and French.[25]

25 *STC2*, nos. 21789.3ff.

The *Meditation on Psalm 50* was transcribed by Meghen, perhaps for Urswick, in Corpus Christi College, Oxford MS 547. A French translation is among the Royal manuscripts in the British Library.[26] They were valued by Luther.[27]

There may just possibly be a connexion with Urswick in a little lavishly illuminated Ghent-Bruges Hours of the Holy Ghost, with prayers for Holy Week, written by Meghen about 1516-7 and now MS 3561 in Lambeth Palace Library (Fig. 10). On the evidence of its calendar, where there is a large number of English saints, it was written for use in England.[28]

It is not at all easy to discern connexions or leading ideas linking the texts within the manuscript miscellanies constructed for Urswick and presumably to his prescription. Connexions with earlier English humanism are sometimes apparent, as in the appearance in Additional MS 15673 and University College, Oxford MS 40 of St John Chrysostom as translated from the Greek by William Sellyng of Canterbury. By and large, however, it is personal piety and the health of the Church that are the most powerful binding factors.

Urswick has served me as a kind of index of what might be called sub-humanist taste and activity in England during the reign of Henry VII and, to some extent, Henry VIII, and in particular of English visual taste for a somewhat coarse style of Netherlandish manuscript, perhaps got a little on the cheap. I want now to look at another late fifteenth-century manifestation of humanism in England, which will take me on to my next lecture, on Thomas More.

I suggested above that Petrarch's laureation on the Capitol in Rome on 8 April 1341 gave an important impulse to the Renaissance movement, and that the oration that he made on the occasion is a document of the first importance for the Renaissance programme of study. A dominant theme in the

26 Royal MS 16 E. XVI, c. 1500.
27 See, in general, Jeremy Musson, *The Development of Reformation Thought and Devotion in England in the Sixteenth and Seventeenth Centuries with particular Reference to the Works of, and those associated with, Fra Girolamo Savonarola (1452-98)*, M.Phil. thesis, London, Warburg Institute, 1989.
28 Christies, *Medieval and illuminated MSS . . .*, London 21 June 1989, lot 37.

oration is the relationship between poetry and history, the rôle of the poet and the historian as preservers. The poets laureate who succeeded Petrarch, as the status gradually became institutionalized, made themselves useful to lay rulers and to prelates in a variety of ways. They celebrated their patrons' achievements in prose and in verse, and they acted as Latin secretaries – as for example Aeneas Sylvius Piccolomini, the future Pope Pius II and the first laureate to receive the distinction outside Italy, did for Frederick III and as Conrad Celtes, the first German laureate, did for Frederick and for Maximilian I.[29] By the time Italian humanism really touches England, in the time of Humfrey, Duke of Gloucester, the Latin poet-historiographer is an integral part of what may loosely be called a court or entourage. Clearly, Tito Livio Frulovisi, for example, was deliberately engaged as a sort of dynastic memorialist. As far as I am aware, however, one does not meet the *de facto* office of historiographer royal in England until the arrival of Bernardus Andreas, Bernard André, the blind Toulousian Augustinian, who may well have been brought to Henry VII's attention by Richard Fox.[30] André perhaps came to England with Henry in 1485, and long remained Henry's client. He wrote in Latin, among other things, Henry's life, and the annals of his reign, as well as an account of Henry's twelve triumphs, in French – a *rifacimento* of the twelve labours of Hercules. André is frequently called laureate, though it is to my mind not by any means sure that he ever was formally crowned – or that anyone was thus honoured in England. If John Skelton was laureated, as his manuscripts and printed editions proclaim, it was abroad, perhaps at Paris or Louvain, where the records are as scanty as the conclusions are unsure.

The England of Henry VII, however, had her experience, both vicarious and actual, of Italians who had undergone formal coronation with bay and been given the title poet laureate. They had made their way here either as papal officials or on diplomatic

29 Trapp, loc. cit. n. 1 above.
30 A convenient summary by G. Tournoy, in *Contemporaries of Erasmus*, i, Toronto 1985, pp. 52–3.

mission. One whose contacts with England were indirect, to say the least, and were chiefly via Erasmus, was Fausto Andrelini of Forlì, student of Pomponio Leto at Rome, and laureated by Leto himself, to whom the privilege had been granted by the Emperor.[31] Admitted to teach poetry at Paris, along with his fellow-laureates Cornelio Vitelli, who was in England before the end of 1489, and Girolamo Balbi, in England in 1493, Andrelini was for twenty years, from 1496, poet royal in France. While Erasmus still had poetic ambitions, he and Andrelini remained friends and so continued until a few years before Andrelini's death in 1518. Besides Vitelli and Balbi, who settled here for some time, England knew other Italian laureates, though there is little or nothing to tell what Englishmen thought of them. According to Polydore Vergil of Urbino, an Italian who long enjoyed English hospitality and was himself a kind of historiographer royal, Henry at least 'was gracious and kind, and was as attentive to his visitors as he was easy of access. His hospitality was splendidly generous; he was fond of having foreigners at his court and freely conferred favours on them', and invited Polydore to compose a history.[32]

A member of the group of Henrician court poets and propagandists was Pietro Carmeliano of Brescia, in England by 1481 after *Wanderjahre*, who opened his campaign for English patronage with a poem on Spring dedicated to Edward Prince of Wales in 1482, and continued it with six hundred hexameters, dedicated to Richard III, on St Catherine of Alexandria. He was tutor to Prince Arthur from 1486 and wrote verses, like his associate Giovanni Gigli, on the marriage of Henry with Elizabeth of York, on the birth of Arthur, and on the betrothal of the

---

31 See G. Tournoy-Thoen, *Contemporaries of Erasmus*, i, 1985, pp.53–56.

32 *The Anglica Historia of Polydore Vergil, A.D. 1485–1537*, ed. with a trans. by Denys Hay, London 1950, pp.xx, 144–5; and see D. Hay, *Polydore Vergil: Renaissance Historian and Man of Letters*, Oxford 1952. See also K. J. Holzknecht, *Literary Patronage in the Middle Ages*, Philadelphia 1923, p.224; G. Kipling, 'Henry VII and the Origins of Tudor Patronage', *Patronage in the Renaissance*, ed. G. F. Lytle and S. Orgel, Princeton 1981, pp.117–8; S. Anglo, 'Ill of the Dead: The Posthumous Reputation of Henry VII', *Renaissance Studies*, i, 1987, pp.27–42.

11 British Library, Additional MS 33736, fols. 1v–2.

Princess Mary to the future Charles V, to expunge the memory of his earlier allegiances (Fig. 11). Carmeliano was Latin Secretary from 1498, and continued as such under Henry VIII for a couple of years before being supplanted by Andrea Ammonio. At the same time as he thus served the English king, Carmeliano was regularly giving intelligence of English matters to Venice.[33] This pattern, too, is far from uncommon.

33 For Carmeliano see M. Firpo, *Dizionario biografico degli italiani*, xx, pp. 410–13 and G. Tournoy, *Contemporaries of Erasmus*, i, Toronto 1985, pp. 270–1; and for Ammonio, id., *Dizionario biografico degli italiani*, xxxvii, pp. 236–41, s.v. Della Rena; id., *Contemporaries of Erasmus*, i, Toronto 1985, pp. 48–50. See also Additional MS 33736, Royal MS 12 A. XXIX, and Oxford, Bodleian Library, Laud MS 501 (Carmeliano) and Harleian MS 336 (Gigli)

Another Italian laureate, but a visitor to England rather than a long-term resident, identified long ago by Francis Wormald,[34] was Johannes Michael Nagonius from the neighbourhood of Pavia. Like the others he was also a minor diplomat, but of a different, more intermittent and itinerant kind. Like the others he was, it seems reasonable to assume, a collector of information for extra-English consumption as well, if in a rather less consistent way. Like them, too, he had an eye to the main chance. Paul Gwynne's study of him, to which I owe most of the information that follows, has shown him to have travelled more widely, both physically and intellectually, than had hitherto been thought.[35] Nagonius addressed laudatory poems in an accomplished italic hand and in slim volumes of something the same style and format as New Year's gifts, to monarchs and magnates all over Europe, frequently, it seems, himself putting the volumes into the hands of their dedicatees, to whom he was often bringing some more exalted state token. To Henry VII he brought such a volume in 1496, along with sword and cap of maintenance from the Pope, staying four months and receiving £30. Nagonius was adept at recycling his verses, which centre on well-worn themes such as ancestry, triumph and prophecy of future greatness. To Henry, the Sibyl promises 'Tu alter Caesar eris . . .', in not particularly distinguished verses that had (most of them), been used already and/or would be used in future for others. The imagery of triumph is deployed at length in poem and picture, as it would later be by Nagonius for Julius II; and so is ancestry, as it is for Louis XII, in the most elaborate and finest of Nagonius's manuscripts.[36]

and G. Tournoy-Thoen, 'Het vroegste Latijnse humanistische Epithalamium in Engeland', *Handelingen van de Koninklijke Zuidnederlandse Maatschappij voor Taal- en Letterkunde en Geschiedenis*, xxxii, 1978, pp.169–80.

34 'An Italian Poet at the Court of Henry VII', *Journal of the Warburg and Courtauld Institutes*, xiv, 1951, pp.118–9.

35 P. G. Gwynne, *The Life and Works of Johannes Michael Nagonius, 'poeta laureatus', c.1450–c.1510*, PhD thesis, London, Warburg Institute, 1990; id., 'Two Latin Poems for Henry VII', *Humanistica Lovaniensia*, forthcoming.

36 Gwynne, op.cit.; R. W. Scheller, 'Imperial Themes in the Art and Literature

The imagery of triumph in England at this time would certainly be worth more study than it has so far received. I speak less of royal entry and progress, ably dealt with by Sydney Anglo,[37] than of the literary-artistic tradition of triumph. This goes back to ancient Rome itself, to the Flavian reliefs, for example, of Marcus Aurelius in triumph, and on to Petrarch and through to Mantegna and beyond. Petrarch's coronation oration makes great play with the entitlement of poets as well as caesars to triumph, but for the visual arts and for literature in general the half-dozen *terza rima* poems, the *Trionfi*, are more directly important. I am speaking here of what one might call diffused, applied, assimilated humanism – often more importantly influential than the stricter, more professional kind, with which it is often combined in the same person.

Petrarch is the case in point. True enough, the learned world admired him for his Latin works of moral instruction, the *De remediis utriusque fortunae* for example; or of humanist virtuosity, the *Bucolicum carmen*, say; or of textual innovation, his constitution of the text of Livy, or his transmission of Cicero's Letters to Atticus, his detection of pretended classical Latin in a document. This admiration extends to the sixteenth century. The presence in that library list that I have mentioned of Petrarch 'in magno volumine' might indicate that the *Opera* of 1501 or 1503 was in question, or one of the moral works; it could equally well, as to format, mean the *Canzoniere* or *Trionfi*. What is said to be Cuthbert Tunstal's copy of the *Canzoniere*, the edition of Venice 1533, with Gesualdo's commentary, incidentally, is now in the Columbia University Library in New York. There is plenty of evidence for the knowledge and circulation of the moral-philosophical works, the *Canzoniere* and the *Trionfi* in England at the time with which we are dealing. One hardly need breathe the names of Thomas Wyatt and the Earl of Surrey.

In introducing Petrarch here, however, I mean to use him in a specific context as an example of assimilated classicism. Strike

of the early French Renaissance: The Period of Charles VIII', *Simiolus*, xii, 1981, pp.27ff.

37 *Spectacle, Pageantry and early Tudor Policy*, Oxford 1969.

12 York Minster Library, MS XVI.N.2, fols. 5v–6.

him anywhere and you hear the ring of ancient bronze. The great sonnet that begins

Hor che 'l ciel e la terra e 'l vento tace . . .

unforgettably set to music by Monteverdi as by many others, is Surrey's

Alas so all things now do hold their peace.

It is also Virgil's great night-piece from *Aeneid* iv, where Dido, betrayed already by Aeneas, has prepared her funeral pyre and is summoning her resolution:

Nox erat et placidum carpebant fessa soporem . . .

The *Trionfi* are also replete with Rome, their personages limited to Antiquity by a deliberate decision, during the revising

Here folowythe dyuers
Balettys and dyties cola-
cyous deuysyd by Mayster Skelton Laureat.

Arboris omne ge
nus viridi conce-
dite lauro.

13 John Skelton, *Dyuers Balettys*, c.1527, Title-page.

process. The *fortuna* of the *Trionfi* among the artists is as varied as it is large, in sophisticated and in naïve media. Processions described in detail are always much easier to illustrate than the images of lyric poetry or the precepts of morality. In volumes of the *Rerum vulgarium fragmenta*, manuscript and printed, illustrations of the *Canzoniere* itself are relatively infrequent. Often enough, there is an opening image of laureation, or of Daphne-Laura, metamorphosed as she flees from Apollo-Petrarch; other illustrations are rarer. Each of the *Trionfi* on the other hand, almost invariably has its introductory picture. Easy to see, behind the image of Henry VII in triumph, drawn by white horses, the Petrarchan Triumph of Love, as adapted in other Italian manuscripts (Fig. 12).

There were endless adaptations of the *Trionfi*, the serial nature of which made them apt for wall-decorations or hangings. Thomas More, for one, in his youth wrote descriptions or *tituli* for painted cloths, tapestry on the cheap, verses for pageants in his father's house, so the 1557 *English Works* declare.[38] Horace Walpole was probably mixing up his monuments when he said More had also written verses for Holbein's *Triumphs of Riches and Poverty* in the London Steelyard. More's early pageants are a curious amalgam of the ages of man and the *Trionfi*. Childhood plays with his top, a young man hawks and hunts, treading down under his horse's feet the child he once was. He in turn is trodden down by Venus and Cupid, who take their stand upon him. An old man sits in his chair, resting his feet upon the conquered goddess and her son, proclaiming old age 'the last and best part of our short life' best employed in helping wisely and discreetly to rule the commonwealth. Then Death spurns the old man's self-satisfaction, and Lady Fame conquers Death, and then Time, with 'horyloge' in hand, triumphs over Fame – and finally the Lady Eternity puts paid to them – and us – all. The programme is reminiscent of that in MS 5066 of the Bibliothèque de l'Arsenal in Paris, containing roughly contem-

38 Ciiir; see my 'Thomas More and the visual Arts', *Saggi sul Rinascimento*, ed. S. Rossi, Milan 1984, pp. 35–6, reprinted in *Essays on the Renaissance and the classical Tradition*, Aldershot 1990, viii, pp. 35–6.

porary designs for tapestry. Upon all this, More makes the Poet moralize *ex cathedra* and significantly in Latin: 'See the vanity of all these things'. Here, no doubt, we have the image of the poet laureate also – something like that image projected by Skelton, or indeed any of the Continental laureates you wish to name (Fig. 13).

II

Erasmus and Thomas More

NOT LONG after he had written his lines for the Poet in his 'pageant', Thomas More wrote a good deal more Latin verse of a rather more accomplished and sophisticated sort. These poems number almost three hundred, and there is additionally a long Latin prose letter defending his accuracy, his poetics and his person against the Frenchman, Germain de Brie, Germanus Brixius.[1] Brixius had written an *Antimorus*, taking More to task for distortion of fact and for metrical lapses, and characterizing him as, among other things, an old bitch (More was thirty-five at the time).

More's Latin poems range in length from two lines to two hundred. More than a hundred of them are translations from the Greek of the Planudean Anthology – such as the one about the man with the long nose who had only to look up at the sun and open his mouth for bystanders to be able to tell the time by the shadow on his teeth. Some of the Anthology translations were made, at an unspecified date, in tandem with William Lily, the

---

1 *Latin Poems*, ed. Clarence H. Miller, Leicester Bradner, Charles Arthur Lynch and Revilo P. Oliver, New Haven and London 1984 = Yale Edition, iii,2. In citing the successive volumes of this comprehensively indexed, indispensable edition, I mean both to indicate my own indebtedness and to refer readers to them for further information.

first High Master of St Paul's School.[2] They selected easy ones, but managed to miss the point of more than one of them. This may have been going on in the 1490s, for Lily may well have returned to England by 1492; and More may have begun his Greek at Oxford, though more likely he was not competent in it until after his return to London, and what seems to have been a period of intensive study with Thomas Linacre from 1499. We know only that More studied Aristotle's *Meteorologica* with Linacre on Linacre's return from Italy after his labours on the Aldine Aristotle.[3] By 1505, More's Greek was secure enough to vie with Erasmus in translating Lucian.[4]

It is not easy to date More's Latin poems. They may well be intermittent productions from the 1490s, say, until almost March 1518, when they were first published, with the intervention of Erasmus, along with *Utopia*, by Johann Froben in Basel. A number of the poems can be dated by the events that called them forth: the epigrams on the coronation of Henry VIII, for example, or the verses that provoked Brixius by mocking his poetic account of the battle between the *Regent*, pride of the English navy, and the *Marie-la-Cordelière*, pride of the French, in which both perished, grappled and in flames. This had happened in the summer of 1512 and Brixius had published his poem in the next year. Similarly datable are the verses on Quentin Massys's diptych of Pieter Gillis and Erasmus of 1517. These, however, are exceptions.

As for the poems' form, the rare hendecasyllables may indicate some influence from Catullus. There is, of course, more from Martial and, for the lyric metres, from the Horace of the *Epodes*; the elegiacs might come from anywhere. Martial and other standard authors for content, too; and Cicero, Seneca, Prudentius, Ausonius; Plutarch's *Moralia*, Diogenes Laertius, Aristotle, Lucian. Some draw on More's favourite Aesopic corpus; some on Renaissance facetists, Poggio Bracciolini and Heinrich Bebel; and there are the usual proverbs and *sententiae*.

2 For Lily, see *Contemporaries of Erasmus*, ii, 1986, pp.329–30.
3 Thomas More, Letter to Dorp, *In Defense of Humanism*, ed. D. Kinney, New Haven and London 1986 = Yale Edition, xv, p.102.
4 Erika Rummel, *Erasmus as a Translator of the Classics*, Toronto 1985, chap. 3.

Spectet, sine omen, non potuit melius.
Principibus nostris uberrima tempora spodet:
& Phoebus radiis & Jouis uxor aquis.

14 British Library, Cotton MS Titus D.IV, fol. 12v.

Originally and startlingly, two are translations of English verna-cular songs. One of these must have run something like: 'My woeful heart plunged in heaviness . . .' and the other certainly began: 'Benedicite, what dreamed I this night/ me thought the world was turned up so down.'

Only very occasionally do we have manuscript evidence for the Latin poems that is more or less contemporary with More, though – as with other works – there are occasional later transcripts. For the epigrams on Massys's diptych, for example, we have a transcript now in Deventer[5] and for the coronation poems we have Cotton MS Titus D. IV in the British Library (Fig. 14).

It has to be admitted that the coronation epigrams are standard flattery, though at least superior to Nagonius. If More is being straightforward, we can take it that the text of the Cotton MS, at least, was transcribed in time for the event which it celebrates, since it is the presentation copy. It is written in an accomplished italic hand and decorated, whether in Britain or in the Low Countries, with a Ghent-Bruges border of similar elegance. More's preface seizes on the problems of producing something worthy of the occasion:

> In attempting, most glorious prince – he opens – to give my clownish verses a better claim to your favour, I hit on applying some colour to them, like a girl who piles the make-up on thick, mistrusting her natural looks. That has made me miss the boat. Of course I wrote them on the dot, but then they had to go to the illuminator, and he could not start at once because of a most inopportune attack of gout. But here they are, at last, so that you can judge whether his hands have been able to make up for the damage his feet have done. My late meed of joy, More goes on – he had read his Suetonius, as we shall see again later – reminds me of how Tiberius put down the Trojans when they brought late condolences on the death of his son: 'Oh thank you,' said he, 'and I was so terribly sorry to hear about what had happened to Hector.' I comfort myself, however, with the thought that I can never be really behindhand, since joy at your accession is everlasting.

5 *Latin Poems*, p.66, illus. between pp.299 and 300.

After this tortuous *captatio benevolentiae*, More launches into his theme: the sudden showers of rain that cannot dampen the pleasure of the day, the tournament for Henry to show his prowess, the new golden age, and an inevitable final flourish of red and white roses. Those Tudor roses have much to answer for. Ten years earlier, when More had put him on the spot, Erasmus had quickly redeemed himself with a rose-trope poem about five little royals growing rosily on the same bush. More's illuminator added the pomegranate for Katherine of Aragon and linked them with the crown, with an extra red rose or two, a fleur-de-lis for the French suzerainty, and the portcullis badge, with the requisite thorns to lacerate the enemies of the realm. More, or his scribe, also identified the topics of panegyric in helpful side-notes.

More's reading debts for the Latin poems have, as I imply above, been very thoroughly traced by the Yale editors, as indeed with the others of More's works in that now monumental edition. Extant evidence, on the other hand, allows us to say little about the books that survive from his library: we must rely almost entirely on inference and extrapolation from his works. A small group can nevertheless be identified. Of manuscripts, he probably owned the twelfth-century St Anselm which is now Royal MS 5 F. IX in the British Library; the Latin grammatical pieces, now Oxford, Bodleian Library, Bodley MS 837; and the chronicles and prophecies concerning England put together in the fourteenth century, now Lambeth Palace Library MS 527; and, among his printed books, the Bodleian has his copy of Euclid's *Elements*, Basel, Johann Herwagen, 1533, presented to More by Simon Grynaeus, its editor, as a thank offering for protection during his visit in England.[6]

Books of devotion, too. Among manuscripts, there must have been the Franco-Flemish book of hours, now in the Cathedral Library at Bamberg.[7] Among the printed books must

6 J. B. Trapp and H. Schulte Herbrüggen, *'The King's good Servant'. Sir Thomas More 1477/8-1535*, Catalogue of the exhibition at the National Portrait Gallery, London, 1977–8, nos. 77–80. This is referred to below as *'King's good Servant'*.

7 H. Schulte Herbrüggen, 'A Prayer-Book of Sir Thomas More', *Times*

In deo laudabo sermones meos: in deo
speraui/nō timebo quid faciat michi caro.
Tota dieuerba mea execrabātur: aduer
sum me oēs cogitationes eorum in malū.
Inhabitabunt et abscondent: ipsi calca
neum meum obseruabunt.
Sicut sustinuerūt aiam meā: p nihilo sal
uos facies illos/in ira populos cōfringes.
Deus vitam meam annunciaui tibi: po
suisti lachrimas meas in conspectu tuo.
Sicut et in promissione tua: tunc conuer
tentur inimici mei retrorsum.
In quacūqz die inuocauero te: ecce cogno
ui quoniam deus meus es.
In deo laudabo verbum/in domino lau
dabo sermonem: in deo speraui/non time
bo quid faciat michi homo.
In me sunt deus vota tua: que reddā lau
dationes tibi.
Quoniā eripuisti animā meā de morte: z
pedes meos de lapsu: vt placeā corā deo
in lumine viuentium. Psalmus.lvj.
Iserere mei deus miserere mei: qm
in te confidit anima mea.
Et in vmbra alarū tuarum sperabo: do
nec transeat iniquitas

15 New Haven, Yale University, Beinecke Library, Thomas More's
Prayer-book, fol. fiiiv.

have been the modest psalter and book of hours, Paris printed, with the record of More's fears and prayers, now at Yale (Fig. 15).[8] This is the profoundly personal and moving record of More's search for protection from those 'demones', the word occurring again and again in the margins, who were tempting his immortal soul to ruin. The words of Psalm 90 reverberate through his work:

> Thou shalt not be afraid for the terror by night; nor for the arrow that flieth by day; nor for the pestilence that walketh in darkness; nor for the destruction that wasteth at noonday . . .

The verse, the sentiments are so familiar, so much a part of More that he can even use them jestingly, lightly, to twit his opponents in controversy with the darkness of their sayings. The terror and the temptations were real, however and they prompted, as well as that repeated word 'demones', the prolonged meditation on the Agony in the Garden, the *De tristitia Christi*.[9] This, the only such substantial holograph of More's still extant, now preserved in the Royal College of Corpus Christi in Valencia (Fig. 16), is unfinished: it must have been in More's possession for the briefest of times, virtually only for the time during which it was written. The Gospel harmony on which it is based, Jean Charlier de Gerson's *Monotessaron*, must surely have been owned by More: he clearly knew it very well indeed.

Among the works relating to the religious controversies of the 1520s and 1530s, there survives, in the British Library, the presentation copy of Johann Eck's *Enchiridion locorum communium adversos Lutheranos* in its second edition of 1526, an exchange, it seems, for a copy of More's own *Responsio ad Lutherum* of

Literary Supplement, 15 January 1970, p.64.
8 *Thomas More's Prayer Book: A Facsimile Reproduction of the annotated Pages*, ed. Louis L. Martz and R. S. Sylvester, New Haven 1969; *'King's good Servant'*, no. 226.
9 Ed. Clarence H. Miller, New Haven and London 1976 = Yale Edition, xiv; *'King's good Servant'*, no.225.

16 Valencia, Royal College and Seminary of Corpus Christi, Holograph MS of Thomas More, *De tristitia Christi*.

1523.[10] Worth mention in this connexion is the *Chronicon* of Cassiodorus, in the edition of 1529, with its admiring dedication to Thomas More by Johannes Cochlaeus, comparing the two senators for richness of learning and readiness to defend the Church.[11] There must have been quantities of the works of the German and the English reformers whom More wrote so much to refute; and Henry VIII's *Assertio septem sacramentorum*, for which More says he was a 'sorter out and placer' of the principal matters – a more modest copy than those printed by Pynson, decorated in a provincial style and bound by John Raynes, the London stationer, for distribution to distinguished recipients.[12] Did More keep file copies of his own works, controversial or

10 *'King's good Servant'*, no. 129.
11 *'King's good Servant'*, no. 128.
12 *Responsio ad Lutherum*, ed. John M. Headley, New Haven and London, 1969 = Yale Edition, v; Nello Vian, 'La presentazione e gli esemplari Vaticani della *Assertio septem sacramentorum* di Enrico VIII', *Collectanea Vaticana in honorem Anselmi M. Card. Albareda*, Vatican City 1962, ii, pp.355–75.

other? We have no means of knowing.[13] The heavy artillery of the 'old holy doctors' as More calls them, the Fathers, especially St Augustine, with whom his work teems, St Cyprian and St Jerome, in Erasmus's editions perhaps – together, of course, with the *Novum Instrumentum* of 1516 and its subsequent re-workings.[14] Family pride would surely have ensured that there was a copy of young John More's only extant work, the translation of Friedrich Nausea on the eucharist of 1533.[15] We have no means of knowing whether More owned Erasmus's Aristotle, too, dedicated to young John,[16] together with Grynaeus's Latin Plato of 1532, though Erasmus had dissuaded Grynaeus from dedicating this to Thomas More, pointing out that such a dedication from a Lutheran, now that More was out of office, might well prove embarrassing. Grynaeus then dedicated to John More his Greek Plato of 1534; a copy would surely have been in the household. Likewise, surely, Margaret Roper's translation of Erasmus's little devotional tract on the Lord's prayer;[17] together with Erasmus's edition of the ps-Ovidian *De nuce*, dedicated to More and his 'school', and his edition of Prudentius's Christmas hymn, dedicated to Margaret at the birth of her first child, and sent with a kiss for the baby; and the translation of Juan Luis Vives *On the Education of Women*, which Thomas More had intended to translate himself, but for lack of time handed over to Richard Hyrde, the tutor.[18] Among secular works, a Chaucer – there are dozens of reminiscences of the first

13 Julian Roberts tells me that none of the works of John Dee – by any account a vainer man than More – appears in the catalogue of his library. See *John Dee's Library Catalogue*, ed. Julian Roberts and Andrew G. Watson, London 1990.

14 See especially Richard C. Marius, 'Thomas More and the early Church Fathers', *Traditio*, xxiv, 1968, pp.379–407; and the relevant volumes of the Yale Edition.

15 'King's good Servant', no. 156.

16 Jill Kraye, 'Erasmus and the Canonization of Aristotle', with an Appendix by M. C. Davies, *England and the Continental Renaissance: Essays in Honour of J. B. Trapp*, ed. Edward Chaney and Peter Mack, Woodbridge 1990, pp.37–52.

17 'King's good Servant', no. 175.

18 'King's good Servant', no. 186.

great English poet in More's English writings; Erasmus's *Apophthegmata* and surely one of Erasmus's main sources, Plutarch, the *Lives* and the *Moralia* – from which came many exemplary anecdotes, such as the one in the *Apology of Sir Thomas More* about the plain-speaking habits of the Macedonians;[19] and the works of Galen, that most frequently printed of all Greek authors in the sixteenth century, equally surely in Linacre's new translations. Perhaps he used Galen in his household, as well as for illustration in his writings, including the *Apology* again – and there is the famous story of how a learned young girl, identified by tradition with More's foster-daughter Margaret Giggs, later the wife of his pupil-servant and Old Pauline John Clement, from her Galen diagnosed a fever which had seized More and prescribed the cure.[20]

No book from More's legal library is extant and I shall attempt no conjectural reconstruction. It is hard to think of him as not knowing the *Corpus iuris civilis*, however, along with the few stand-bys of the English common lawyer, the latter chiefly manuscript digests and abridgements of case law. One may hope that More was an honourable exception to the norm of intellectual narrowness apparent in such luminaries as Thomas Keble about the turn of the century.[21] His knowledge of canon law must surely have been at least as good as another English lawyer's, for he could argue points in it on at least equal terms with pamphlet antagonists of the 1530s such as Christopher St German, author of *Doctor and Student*.[22] He could use familiarity

---

19 Ed. J. B. Trapp, New Haven and London 1979 = Yale Edition, ix, p.42.

20 More, *Dialogue of Comfort against Tribulation*, ed. Louis L. Martz and Frank Manley, New Haven and London 1976 = Yale Edition, xii, pp.368–9.

21 See R. J. Schoeck, 'The Libraries of Common Lawyers in Renaissance England. Some Notes and a provisional List', *Manuscripta*, vi, 1962, pp.155–67; and especially E. W. Ives, 'A Lawyer's Library in 1500', *Law Quarterly Review*, lxxxv, 1969, pp.104–116. I thank Professor J. H. Baker for his advice in this regard.

22 For St German, see most recently J. A. Guy's contributions to Thomas More, *The Debellation of Salem and Bizance*, New Haven and London 1987 = Yale Edition, x; and J. H. Baker's Introduction to *Doctor and Student*, Birmingham, Alabama 1988. See also R. J. Schoeck, 'Common Law and

to satiric effect, for example in affecting to despise St German as the poor little parish priest or timid religious recluse he pretended to believe him to be, by scorning the confessors' manuals, the *Summa Rosella* and the like, that St German had cited in support of his arguments.

Turning to the humanism and the books of my title, one may perhaps be able to say something of More's historical armoury. Of modern works, he cites – as *Cronica Cronicarum* – the *Liber Cronicarum* of Hartmann Schedel, the famous *Nuremberg Chronicle*;[23] and among church historians he clearly knew Platina and his *Vitae pontificum*.[24] The historians that Hythlodaye took to Utopia were Plutarch, Thucydides, Herodotus and Herodian – all in Greek, which the Utopians are characterized as appreciating so highly. More's own tastes among the ancient historians was rather for the Latins, Sallust, Livy, Tacitus and Suetonius.

Livy was a favourite and there is a number of verbal reminiscences of that historian in More's Latin works. Manlian rules of law, applications of law that ignore all humanity and equity, for example, are mentioned in the marginal notes to *Utopia*. Later, Erasmus wrote to Guillaume Budé, the great French scholar and More's friend, that Livy was in the hands of More's household, day and night.[25] Livy is the storehouse of good phrase and example. In his *Apology* of 1533, More tells the story of how, in the time of Hannibal, a stratagem was employed in Capua by one Pacuvius Calanius to demonstrate to the populace how difficult it was to choose good governors. He gives the reference very precisely and there can be no doubt that he took it direct from Livy, though the sense in which he takes it is not the same as Livy's.[26] But what text of Livy did he use? The form of the name Calanius may give a clue. It is the form regularly used in

Canon Law in their Relation to Thomas More', *St Thomas More: Action and Contemplation*, ed. R. S. Sylvester, New Haven 1972, pp.15–56.

23 R. J. Schoeck, in *Bulletin of the Institute of Historical Research*, xxxv, 1962, pp.84–6.

24 e.g. Thomas More, *Debellation*, ed. cit., pp.282–3.

25 Letter 1233, 1521; Allen, iv, p.577; *Correspondence*, viii, p.296.

26 Ed. J. B. Trapp, London and New Haven, 1979 = Yale Edition, ix, pp.79–82.

editions up to the Aldine, of which the second volume, where the story occurs, was published in 1519. The Aldine reading 'Calauius' becomes standard thereafter. Is the inference that More continued to use virtually until the end of his life the Livy he had bought much or even only a little earlier than 1519 – or are we dealing only with a turned letter? 'Calauius' is the reading of More's *English Works* of 1557.

Livy has little or no relevance to the monarchical subject matter of More's own *Historia Richardi Tertii*, which exists both in Latin and in English. We know tantalizingly little about *Richard III*, that prime document in the formation of the Tudor image – myth or reality according to taste – of Richard Crookback, though our knowledge has recently been augmented by the discovery of another manuscript.[27] We cannot even be sure when it was written or when it was perhaps revised. The writing may well have been early and the revisions made between 1513 and 1518. Certainly the blackness of Richard's portrait might have seemed less relevant to the conditions of the 1510s than those of the 1490s, say. There is also the problem of the factual sources. If Archbishop Morton, that prop of Henry VII, was chief among them, he must have imparted his information to the young More, since he died in 1500. The *Dictionary of National Biography* says starkly that Morton wrote the *History*. If he did, More had waited rather long to put his old patron's work into print. In any case, his boyhood time in Morton's household must have been passed in the late 1480s or early 1490s. Christopher Urswick was available with reminiscence over there in Hackney still until 1522; and Richard Fox, Bishop of Winchester and Privy Seal, with whom More was in close contact – there are legal instruments signed by both – in the decade when, by common consent, the Latin version was produced in the form in which we have it. There were others, Pietro Carmeliano among them, whom More satirized along with Bernard André

27 *The History of King Richard III*, ed. Richard S. Sylvester, New Haven and London 1963 = Yale Edition, ii; and, for the new text, *In Defense of Humanism*, ed. D. Kinney, New Haven and London 1986 = Yale Edition, xv, pp.314–85, 605–31.

(dispraise of his father seems not to have been entirely unwelcome to Henry VIII.) Domenico Mancini's *De occupatione Regni Angliae* may have been available in manuscript: it was not printed until 1936. Likewise, there was Polydore Vergil's *Anglica Historia*, also available to More, if at all, in manuscript.[28] What I have to say centres on the Latin, and its implication is that More is a more fundamentally humanist historian than either Mancini or Polydore in the way he uses his classical models. The Italians are, paradoxically, annalists rather than historians. More's familiar friends among the ancient Roman historians are, in this instance, Sallust, Tacitus and Suetonius, all amply available in print. Sallust was recommended by More himself as basic reading for his 'school',[29] and there are verbal echoes of Sallust throughout the work, not to mention the use of the noble whore Sempronia as a model for Jane Shore, and the reminiscences of Catiline in the portrait of Richard. More influential in this, however, is the Tiberius of Tacitus and Suetonius. We have already seen More using Suetonius's Tiberius in elaborate compliment to Henry. At the other end of the scale is the horrifying story which he took out of Suetonius or out of Tacitus and, according to William Roper, told the Bishops of Durham, Bath and Winchester when they invited him to accompany them to the coronation of Anne Boleyn in 1533.[30] More may have been up-to-date enough to have read his Tacitus in Beroaldus's new edition of 1515, the *Annals* in any case not being available until then. William Grocyn had a copy, and John Dorne the Oxford bookseller stocked him in the early 1520s; Linacre and Polydore Virgil used him for *exempla*.

Among Greek authors, there can be no doubt that More's favourite was Lucian, in earlier days at least. The witty Syrian rhetorician, set to 'drive and whoop idolatry out of the world' and show 'all the gods and goddesses to be no better than a

28 Mancini was edited by C. A. J. Armstrong, Oxford 1936; 2nd. ed. Oxford 1969; Virgil by D. Hay, London 1950.
29 Letter to William Gonell, *Correspondence*, ed. Elizabeth Frances Rogers, Princeton 1947, no. 63, p.123.
30 William Roper, *The Lyfe of Sir Thomas Moore, knighte*, ed. E. V. Hitchcock, London 1935, pp.58–9.

company of gypsies' looks a rather uncharacteristic choice for someone who was later to be so much involved with defence of his Church's views, but More's letter to Ruthall, quoted below, gives a hint at his attraction. Lucian had been familiar in the West since Guarino and Aurispa had brought manuscripts from Constantinople; he was translated and printed in Latin from 1470 onwards, and he was imitated almost without end. The Greek *editio princeps* was issued at Florence in 1496, and Aldus – whom More's Utopians appreciate so much for his Greek productions – printed him in 1503. One of the finest Renaissance manuscripts in the British Library was presented to Henry VIII in 1519: three of Lucian's dialogues in the Latin of Livio Guidolotti of Urbino, with some of the Lucianic apologues of Pandolfo Collenuccio of Pesaro (1444–1504), written in Italy between 1509 and 1517 to a commission by one Geoffrey Chamber by the great Lodovico degli Arrighi and illuminated by Attavante degli Attavanti, the leading Florentine book-painter of his day (Fig. 17).[31] The Yale editor of More's Lucian translations states the problem: More's early appreciation of Lucian's wit, humour, common-sense, hatred of sham and exposure of it are hardly something to which he could have given full approval in later life, as the man who would have burned Erasmus's *Praise of Folly* – than which no work is more Lucianic, except perhaps *Utopia* – and his own works rather than that they should harm the faith.

More was Lucian's first English translator, into a discreet and learned Latin. His translations were popular enough, appearing at least nine times before More's death in 1535, which means that they were reprinted more often than *Utopia*.[32] They were almost certainly made in 1505 or early 1506. More had been working hard at his Greek since 1501 at the latest and had achieved a good degree of competence though, in writing his own declamation in reply to Lucian's *Tyrannicida*, he used Latin alone.

31 Royal MS 12 C. VIII.
32 *Translations of Lucian*, ed. Craig R. Thompson, New Haven and London 1974 = Yale Edition iii,1.

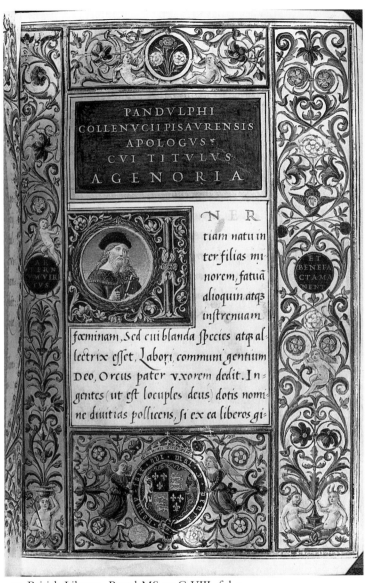

PANDVLPHI
COLLENVCII PISAVRENSIS
APOLOGVS:
CVI TITVLVS·
AGENORIA

NER
tiam natu in
ter filias mi
norem, fatuã
alioquin atqz
inſtrenuam
fœminam, Sed cui blanda ſpecies atqz al
lectrix eſſet, Labori, communi gentium
Deo, Orcus pater vxorem dedit. In=
gentes (ut eſt locuples deus) dotis nomi=
ne diuitias pollicens, ſi ex ea liberos gi

17 British Library, Royal MS 12 C.VIII, fol.4.

The translations are prefaced by a dedicatory letter to Thomas Ruthall. 'Humanissime Ruthall', as Erasmus addressed him elsewhere, was another of those Tudor ecclesiastics and royal servants, like Urswick, Fox and Tunstal, the last of whom was to succeed him at one remove as Bishop of Durham: royal secretary in 1499, Dean of Salisbury in 1502, from 1503 Chancellor of Cambridge University and Archdeacon of Gloucester, ambassador, Privy Councillor from 1516 – about the same time as Colet and More – and from 1509 until his death in 1523 Bishop of Durham. In the dedication More writes of the delight and instruction to be got from Lucian, who is the model moral censor, not arrogant like the philosophers or wanton like the poets, but skilful in thrusting deep without wounding. Moreover, he was much approved by earlier and therefore better Christians, such as St John Chrysostom. Chrysostom put a large part of Lucian's *Cynicus* into one of his homilies, attracted by its praise of the severe Cynic life, which he found comparable with true Christianity in its simplicity, temperance and frugality. In other words, More is occupying and defending the Christian humanist position taken by Erasmus – though not (as we shall see) by Colet, their friend. The *Necromantia* is admirable, More goes on, for its witty rebuke of deceit, whether by magicians or poets, and its criticism of the contendings among philosophical sects. And there is the *Philopseudes*, with its castigation of lying so well expressed and effective that one need not be troubled by its pagan doubting of the soul's immortality, and can take to heart what it commands us to do: shun superstition and avoid anxiety. Strange stuff, all this. So is what comes next, in the shape of strong criticism of hell-fire sermons and invented saints' legends, from which More goes on to plead for a more rational, intelligent, thinking Christianity, a Christianity which should not, does not, need the support of old wives' tales. Here he is tilting at the same sort of thing as he is in the later, so-called 'humanistic letters' of 1515–19, to Maarten van Dorp and the unnamed monk, whom we now know to have been John Batmanson, making fun of the sort of story which he had found current in Coventry. There it had been put about that praying the rosary would get you clear of the consequences of sin, so that the locals were sinning mightily and fingering their beads by turns.[33] There is a perfect consistency between this position and More's position in the later works of controversy with the English heretics concerning devotion to the saints: abuse alone need not invalidate. It is right to venerate images for the reality that lies behind them. This is good and commanded by the tradition of the Church. What is stupid, and what has nothing to do with true worship and real Christianity is to offer oats to the image of the bearded lady, the mythical St Wilgefortis, St Uncumber, in St Paul's Cathedral, as silly women do to cause their husbands not to molest them in bed.[34]

That Lucian lies behind both *The Praise of Folly*, which was written down, it seems, in More's house and dedicated to him in fellow-Lucianity, and *Utopia* will hardly be disputed. A copy or copies surely must have formed part of his library. I shall touch on it later in the context of the dispute over the *Novum Instrumentum*. It is also closely related to More's *Utopia*.

Were one to set out on an analysis of *Utopia* in terms of the books and authors to which and to whom More has been held to be indebted in the making of it, the quest would be never-ending. Had More read them all, he would never have had time to write. The printing history of the book itself is fairly simple, if a little curious. First published by Dirk Martens at Louvain at the end of 1516, on the recommendation of Erasmus, and seen through the press by More's friend Pieter Gillis, pensionary of Antwerp (Yale has Tunstal's copy); then Paris 1517, like the first edition an undistinguished little object which young Thomas

---

33 *In Defense of Humanism. Letter to Martin Dorp, Letter to the University of Oxford, Letter to Edward Lee, Letter to a Monk*, ed. D. Kinney, New Haven and London 1986 = Yale Edition, xv, pp.284–8.

34 See especially *A Dialogue concerning Heresies*, ed. T. M. C. Lawler, G. Marc'hadour, and R. C. Marius, New Haven and London 1981 = Yale Edition, vi; but also, in particular, *The Confutation of Tyndale's Answer*, ed. L. A. Schuster, R. C. Marius, J. P. Lusardi and R. J. Schoeck, New Haven and London 1973 = Yale Edition, viii; *Letter to Bugenhagen, Supplication of Souls, Letter against Frith*, ed. F. Manley, G. Marc'hadour, R. C. Marius and C. H. Miller, New Haven and London 1990 = Yale Edition, vii; and cf. *Apology* and *Debellation*, ed.cit.

18 Thomas More, *Utopia*, Basel 1518.

Lupset was supposed to have looked after; then the two editions, accompanied by More's *Epigrammata*, which were the responsibilty of Erasmus and were published from Froben's press in Basel in March and December 1518 (Fig.18); then, significantly enough with the Lucian translations, at Florence in 1519. Then what happens? Had the joke gone stale? Or were successive reprints made without alteration of title-page? At all events, there is no further Latin edition until that of Louvain in 1548, the same year as the Italian translation. The Italian had been preceded by a German translation of the second book, the description of the Utopian commonwealth only, in 1524. Then, after the Italian, the French, in 1550. Then a spurt of Latins in Cologne, Basel and Louvain, including some printings included in the Latin *Opera* in the 1550s and 1560s, English by Ralphe Robynson in 1551 – twice reprinted in the decade of Mary – and Dutch about the same time, but Spanish not until 1637. No new English translation before that of Gilbert Burnet in 1684, a revision of Robynson.

Robynson gives an engaging self-portrayal as Diogenes the Cynic in his philosopher's cloak, rolling his tub up and down so as not to appear idle when all others in the commonwealth were busy to strengthen it, working ineffectually, he told Cecil, to translate this eloquent, fruitful and profitable book, with its blueprint for the best variety of state. *Utopia*, he goes on, in the best Edwardian vein, is a remarkable work to have been written by one so blinded to the 'shining light of Godes holy truthe in certain pointes of Christian religion.' Robynson's preface also contains the obligatory vernacular humanist's apology for the rudeness of the native tongue, which Bishop Burnet later takes up in the spirit of his later times.[35] Dryden had found Chaucer a rough diamond, who must be polished ere he shines. Burnet notes that 'the French took no ill method, when they intended to reform and beautify their language, in setting their best writers to work to translate the Greek and Latin authors into it'

35 R. F. Jones, *The Triumph of the English Language: A Survey of Opinions concerning the Vernacular from the Introduction of Printing to the Restoration*, Stanford 1953.

and he finds that now our own language 'is more natural and proper, than it was ever at any time before.'[36]

Burnet's view of *Utopia* is remarkable for the way in which he hits the point while missing it by miles. To him the second book is so out of character, with its ban on private property, its naked pre-marital mutual inspections, its hired assassins – 'so wild and so immoral both, that it does not admit of anything to soften or excuse it, much less to justify it.' The 'tenderest part', he felt, and the part most in earnest was the 'dialogue of counsel' in the first book, in which, Burnet believed, having experience of the court himself, More was writing of the father's court to the son: Henry VII's court was being described to Henry VIII.

That famous 'dialogue of counsel', More's debate with himself about whether to serve or to remain a private person has, of course, a long history in philosophical and sub-philosophical texts from antiquity to the Renaissance, which there is no space to trace here. More met it young, as we shall see, in Pico della Mirandola. For him, as later for John Milton, there was never really any escape from that stark Ciceronian active humanist imperative: worth resides in action. The 'dialogue of counsel', too, has affinities with the *Aula*, *The Court*, of the rackety Franconian knight Ulrich von Hutten, as Hutten himself had seen when he wrote soon after its publication in 1518 to Erasmus to know what sort of man was this Thomas More, author of *Utopia* and, Hutten had heard, an admirer. The wonderful letter that Erasmus wrote in reply during 1519, affectionate and carefully wrought, is the basis of most people's view of Thomas More. It cannot too often be said that this is not the Thomas More of the days after he had realized the nature of the Lutheran threat, the More of the 1520s and 1530s.[37]

Burnet was right in principle about *Utopia*, even though he misses the point. The first book is serious; the second a joke, but a joke that is also *salutaris*. It carries on, in its Lucianic paradoxical framework, the framework of the journey from this world to the next, from the Old to the New, from corruption

36 Preface to *Utopia*.
37 Letter 999; Allen, iv, pp. 12–23; *Correspondence*, vii, pp. 15–25.

to natural goodness – but also from grace to nature – some at least of the first book. How to deal with thieves, for example: the attitudes of Books I and II are perfectly consistent.

Nothing written above, of course, is intended to deny that *Utopia* is full of More's reading as well as his wit. You may follow that through many modern books and the full and painstaking commentary of the Yale *editio maior*.[38] There are some things, inevitably, that even such an edition will not tell you – and Paul Turner's quite admirable modern Penguin translation will. That the pre-marital inspection comes out of Horace, for example: you look thoroughly at a piece of horse-flesh before you buy, says Horace; why go more blindly into marriage? And those golden chamber-pots which teach little Utopians to despise gold and riches have been shown to come out of Plutarch's *Moralia*.[39] Perhaps those great golden chains for slaves find an echo in a contemporarily perceived English love of massy golden display. More himself, Erasmus tells us in the letter to Hutten, had a distaste for such adornments, except when propriety demanded that they be worn – as, one must presume, when he sat to Holbein for the superb portrait which is now in the Frick Collection in New York (Fig.19). In 1514, a little, perhaps, before More was granted the collar of SS that proclaimed him Henry's man, at a moment when Henry VIII in his turn was being given the sword and ceremonial cap by the Pope, an Italian visitor remarked on the massive gold chains worn by English noblemen, so heavy that they might have served for fetters on a felon's ankles, valuable for their weight and not their workmanship.[40]

Utopian slaves are slaves to gold in a special sense. The book itself is, among other things, an investigation of how all are similarly in thrall. Its heart is the great problem of grace and nature, but More keeps continually before us that other great problem of *meum et tuum*, most clearly defined in the second

38 *Utopia*, ed. E. Surtz and J. H. Hexter, New Haven and London 1965 = Yale Edition, iv.
39 J. Duncan M. Derrett, *Moreana*, lxxiii, 1982, pp.75–6.
40 Marino Sanudo, *Diarii*, xviii, 12 July 1514, Venice 1887, col. 352.

19 Hans Holbein the Younger, Portrait of Thomas More, 1527. New York, Frick Collection.

book. Long ago, in 1517 to be precise, Guillaume Budé and others saw this, and put it into their liminary commendations.[41] There is no reason to think that More did not mean Utopian communism to be taken seriously, whether he had arrived at his valuation of such a system by analogy with monastic communities or not.

Utopia is a book from which you may take almost any lesson you wish. As its first title-page proclaims, it concerns the best state of a commonwealth, a truly golden book, as diverting as it is wholesome and as wholesome as it is pleasant, which seems to mean that we are to take it in the Horatian sense as truthful in jest. In the end, too, the whole depends on the hoary old paradox of the negative: nothing, nobody, nowhere. The nobody joke stretches from Homer's *Odyssey*, where it is part of the trickster's armoury: for his ruse-escape from Polyphemus, Odysseus is *Outis*, Nobody; but he is also showing that he is *Metis*, Nobody, as well as justifying his own epithet, *polymetis*, alert and ever-ready. The joke resurfaces in medieval mock-sermons in praise of St Nobody – solemnly condemned by solemn churchmen at Paris in 1277 – in Reformation imagery, in Elizabethan-Jacobean drama, including *The Tempest*, in children's rhymes and caricatures in our own day (Fig.20).[42] Not much of a joke, perhaps, but a lasting one. If you ask where all these things happen, where all is natural, rational, pious and orderly, the answer is precisely: in Utopia, which is to say Nowhere.

In Utopia, too, ancient Greek studies are valued at the proper level, a level which More had a little later, in 1518, to reprove the University of Oxford for failing to reach.[43] Raphael Hythlodaye, the Portuguese voyager who tells the tale of the island, is himself represented as having been a student of philosophy, and all the best philosophy was in Greek, except for bits of Cicero and Seneca. Hythlodaye took Greek philosophy books to Utopia,

---

41 Reprinted in the Yale Edition, iv, pp.2–37.
42 G. Calmann, 'The Picture of Nobody', *Journal of the Warburg and Courtauld Institutes*, xxiii, 1960, pp.60–104.
43 *In Defense of Humanism* = Yale Edition, xv, 1986, pp.129–50, 544–52.

20 Hans Weiditz, *Nobody*, 1518.

finding – as men were accustomed to do at the time – that the local vernacular had affinities with the ancient tongue.[44] The books were highly appreciated, even in their mutilated state: the ship's pet monkey had torn some pages out of Theophrastus on plants. Even so, the Utopians got most of Plato, some Aristotle as well, but Lascaris's grammar only, because for some reason Theodore Gaza's was not taken. For dictionaries, only Hesychius and Dioscorides. Dioscorides's appearance here is curious and – for me, at least – not easily explainable. Though the *Materia medica* is a conscious attempt to be encyclopaedic, its arrangement is systematic and not alphabetical. Still, as a *livre de consultation* on its subject, it had no rival. The Utopians loved Plutarch – whether the *Lives* or the *Moralia* is not made plain. Both perhaps, with an emphasis on the latter. And Lucian, of course, for his wit and pleasantry. Aristophanes, Homer, Euripides and Sophocles, the best edition, in the small Aldine type. That would be the second, quarto Aldine edition, just out when More was writing. Thucydides and Herodotus among the classical historians, with Herodian for the later period. Emphasis on Greek, with a characteristic humanist predilection for poetry, history and moral philosophy, is strongly marked. There is a tincture of medicine, again in Greek, from Hippocrates to the *Microtegni* of Galen – though the healthy Utopians are not in much need of physic.

The Utopians were quick to pick up other European advantages. Shown the productions of Aldus Manutius, they soon cottoned on and began industrious experiments. Hitherto knowing only tree-bark, parchment and papyrus, they were soon able to make paper and, after few failures, were able to print. All that was now holding them back was a shortage of copy-texts, especially of those desirable Greek authors. Even so, they had struck off many thousands of copies.

Whether the accuracy of Utopian printing was improved by the difficulty of cutting, casting and setting Greek type, More

---

44 A sketch in J. B. Trapp, 'The "Conformity" of Greek with the Vernacular: The History of a Renaissance Theory of Languages', *Essays on the Renaissance and the classical Tradition*, Aldershot 1990, i, pp.8–21.

does not tell us. Perhaps it was. More himself believed that the extra effort required to form Greek characters and the extra care that scribes were therefore obliged to take as they transcribed Greek manuscripts, particularly of the New Testament, made for greater textual accuracy. As a general rule in copyists this is open to doubt, but for More it was ammunition in the war against conservative theologians.[45] The theologians' defence of the Vulgate, muddied though it might have been by centuries of translation and transmission but – as they held – purified by the sanction of the Church rather than from the untainted, silver springs of the original Greek so greatly valued by More, Colet and Erasmus, had to be broken.

The fellow-work of three friends in the battle to break it is summed up in the imitation books in a pledge of friendship which More received within a few months of the publication of *Utopia*. In May 1517, Erasmus and Pieter Gillis commissioned from the foremost Antwerp portrait-painter of the day, Quentin Massys, a diptych consisting of portraits of themselves to send to their English associate. They got something revolutionary: the active and the contemplative humanist life personified on panel (Figs.21–22).[46] Erasmus made this explicit: he was always the spokesman. We hear little or nothing directly from Gillis, though More took care to acknowledge the gift to both. Gillis, indeed, holds a letter addressed to him in More's hand. This, as far as I know, is an innovation. There are many pictures, especially Flemish pictures, in which books and papers figure, even letters, identifying interests or profession. The extra detail of a letter from the very man to whom the portrait was to be

45 'Letter to Dorp', *In Defense of Humanism*, 1986, pp.92–3.
46 L. Campbell, Margaret M. Phillips, H. Schulte Herbrüggen and J. B. Trapp, 'Quentin Matsys, Desiderius Erasmus, Pieter Gillis and Thomas More', *Burlington Magazine*, cxx, 1978, pp.716–25; and 'Postscript', ibid., cxxi, 1979, pp.436–7; J. B. Trapp, 'La iconografia de Santo Tomás Moro', *Lecturas de historia del arte*, ii, 1990, pp.47–50. A parallel and almost exactly contemporary case of reference to the sitter through the book shown is Raphael's portrait of Leo X with Cardinals Giulio de' Medici and Luigi de' Rossi in the Uffizi, where the Hamilton Bible is shown open at the beginning of St John's Gospel.

given is something new by way of specific personal reference. More's letter of thanks begs back the letter shown in the portrait, so that it can be put up beside it and double the effect of the miracle the painter has wrought in his imitation of reality. As he holds More's letter, Gillis is surrounded by Erasmian reference. His right forefinger rests on Erasmus's *Antibarbari*, the unfinished work not in fact printed until 1522. Perhaps it was well enough known to be put into a picture; or perhaps the title was added later, even very much later, to accord with the legends on the books in the portrait of Erasmus, which must have been there when the portrait was painted, since the rubric to More's letter refers to them. The addition of such legends, if they are additions, to the portrait of Gillis could have been made as late as the late seventeenth or eighteenth century, at the time when it was enlarged to make a (false) pair with Holbein's portrait of Erasmus. They do not have quite the same close reference to More or to Gillis as do those on the portrait of Erasmus, either for More or for the sitter. Gillis had edited the letters of Poliziano and the *Opuscula* of Rudolph Agricola, as well as a Latin Aesop and a couple of collections of Erasmus's letters by the time the portrait was painted, but there is no sign of them.[47] There are only works by Erasmus, and even these bear the marks of barrel-scraping, being chiefly rather minor and lacking in specific personal reference. There is, certainly, the *Antibarbari*; and there is the *Education of a Christian Prince*, in then fashionable Greek disguise as *Archontopaideia*. The *Christian Prince* was certainly one of Erasmus's most famous and influential productions. Addressed to the young man who would become Roman Emperor as Charles V, it was liberally distributed among European crowned heads. The fine vellum presentation copy for Henry VIII is now at Charlecote Park, Warwickshire.[48] The others are Plutarch (probably), Suetonius

47 A good summary account of Gillis by M. A. Nauwelaerts, *Contemporaries of Erasmus*, ii, Toronto 1986, pp.99–101.

48 Cecil H. Clough, 'A presentation Volume for Henry VIII: The Charlecote Park Copy of Erasmus's *Institutio principis*', *Journal of the Warburg and Courtauld Institutes*, xliv, 1981, pp.199–202.

21 Quentin Massys, Portrait of Erasmus as St Jerome, 1517. Hampton Court.

22 Quentin Massys, Portrait of Pieter Gillis, 1517. Private Collection.

and Quintus Curtius, all authors with whom Erasmus had concerned himself about this time, but with a general relevance only to the occasion and to the persons involved.

With Erasmus, the focus is much sharper. Massys fixes the image of Erasmus that was to endure, of Erasmus at work, the image that Erasmus himself must have prescribed. The likeness that Massys made for his medal of Erasmus is static, despite the defiant affirmation by the god Terminus on the reverse. On the panel, alive with intellectual energy, it is dynamic. Dürer must have known both painted portrait and medal – though he also drew Erasmus from the life. Holbein also, perhaps; or are his portraits of Erasmus at his desk, in Basel and the Louvre, reinventions of the formula? Erasmus is shown writing, with the reed pen he preferred to the quill because it suited his rapid, cursive hand. He is, moreover, shown writing, in an excellent facsimile of that hand, the very work that he was writing in May 1517, when the portrait was commissioned.[49] This was his Paraphrase of Romans. Though recent cleaning has shown that it is not the keyword of the Epistle, 'gratia', grace, that appears on the verso page of the manuscript before him, there is no doubt of what is meant. As the rubric to the Deventer transcript and the printed version of More's letter of thanks say, Erasmus is writing and the books on the shelves display their titles, and they all emphasize the bonds between More and Erasmus: Greek and true theology. The Lucian is a reference to their joint work. There is also the *Moriae encomium*, the *Praise of Folly*, in which – as Erasmus himself put it in his preface – 'our common interests' are served. Conceived, so Erasmus said, as he rode over the Alps towards his third visit to England, it was written, it seems, in Thomas More's house in Bucklersbury, in the city of London. Later, Erasmus said rightly that it was really the *Enchiridion militis christiani* in paradoxical, ironic, inverted form. More, its dedicatee, was the person best qualified, by tempera-

49 A further substantial witness to Erasmus's handwriting, in its form of ten years or so later, has just passed through the London sale-rooms, in the shape of his personal copy of the *Adagia*, Basel 1523, heavily annotated in preparation for later editions; see Sotheby's Catalogue of Continental and Russian Books and Manuscripts, 20 November 1990, lot 397.

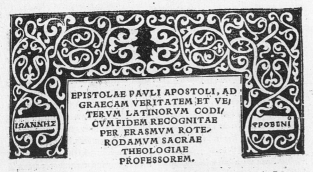

**EPISTOLAE PAVLI APOSTOLI, AD
GRAECAM VERITATEM ET VE/
TERVM LATINORVM CODI/
CVM FIDEM RECOGNITAE
PER ERASMVM ROTE/
RODAMVM SACRAE
THEOLOGIAE
PROFESSOREM.**

ΙΩΑΝΝΗΣ   ΦΡΟΒΕΝΙ

ΠΑΥΛΟΥ ΤΟΥ ΑΠΟΣΤΟΛΟΥ Η
ΠΡΟΣ ΡΩΜΑΙΟΥΣ ΕΠΙΣΤΟΛΗ

ΑΥΛΟΣ δ῾Υ͂λος πα
ΣΟΥ ΧΡΙΣΤΟΥ, κλη/
Τὸς ἀπόσολος,ἀφω/
ρισμένος ἐις ἐυαγγέλι
ον θεῦ,ὃ προεπηγγεί/
λατο διὰ Τῶν προφη
τῶν αὐτ̃ ἐν γραφαῖς ἁ/
γίαις,περὶ τ̃ ἱοῦ αὐτ̃,
τ̃ γενομἐνου ἐκ σπέρματος Δαβίδ, καΤὰ σάρκα,
τ̃ ὁρισθέντος ἱοῦ θεῦ,ἐν δυνάμει, καΤὰ πνευ/
μα ἀγιωσύνης, ἐξ ἀνασάσεως νεκρῶν, ΙΗΣΟΥ
ΧΡΙΣΤΟΥ τ̃ κυρίε ἡμῶν,δι' ὃυ ἐλάβομεν χά/
ριν καὶ ἀπosολίὡ ,ἐις ὑπακοἱὼ πίστεως ἐν
πᾶσι τοῖς ἔθνεσιν, ὑπὲρ τ̃ ὀνόματος αὐτ̃,
ἐν οἷς ἐσὲ καὶ ὑμε̃ς, κληΤοὶ ΙΗΣΟΥ ΧΡΙΣΤΟΥ,
πᾶσι τοῖς οὖσιν ἐν ῥώμῃ,ἀγαπητοῖς θεῦ, κλη/
τοῖς ἁγίοις . χάρις ὑμῖν ἢ ἐιρήνη ἀπὸ θεῦ
πατρὸς ἡμῶν, ηαὶ κυρίε ΙΗΣΟΥ ΧΡΙΣΤΟΥ.
πρῶτον μὲν ἐυχαριστῶ τῷ θεῷ με,διὰ ΙΗ
ΣΟΥ ΧΡΙΣΤΟΥ,ὑπὲρ πάντων ὑμῶν,ὅτι ἡ πί/
στις ἡμῶν καταγγέλλεται ἐν ὅλῳ τῷ κόσμῳ.
μάρτυς γάρ μου ἐsὶν ὁ θεὸς,ᾧ λατρέυω ἐν τῷ
πνέυματί με , ἐν τῷ ἐυαγγελίῳ τῷ ἱοῦ αὐτ̃,
ὡς ἀδιαλείπτως μνέαν ὑμῶν ποιῦμαι πάν/
τε ἐπὶ τ̃ προσευχῶν με,δεόμϸος,ἐιπως ἤδη
ποτὲ ἐυοδωθήσομαι ἐν τῷ θελήμαΤι τῦ θεῦ
ἐλθεῖν

*κεφάλαι-
ον δεύτε-
ρον*

EPISTOLA PAVLI APO/
STOLI AD ROMANOS.

AVLVS SERVVS Iesu Christi,uocat⁹ apłs,segregatus in euãgeliũ dei,quod ante promiserat per pphetas suos, in scripturis sanctis de filio suo,q genit⁹ fuit ex semine Da uid,secũdũ carnē,qui declarat⁹ fuit fili⁹ dei,in potētia,secũdũ spiritũ sanctifica tiõis,ex eo q resurrexit a mortuis Iesu christus dñs noster, per quē accepim⁹ gratiã & muneris apłici functionē, ut obediat fidei inter oēs gentes,sup ipsi us noie, quorꝝ de numero estis & uos, uocati Iesu Christi,omnib⁹ qui Romæ estis,dilectis dei,uocatis sãctis, Gratia uobis & pax a deo patre nostro,& dño Iesu Christo.   Primũ qdē gratias ago deo meo,p Iesum Christũ,super oibus uobis, quod fides uestra annunciat in toto mundo.Testis eni meus est deus, cui seruio in spiritu meo,in euãgelio fi lij sui,quod indesinenter mentione ue stri facio,semp in orationibus meis de precãs, si quo modo tandem aliquã/ do,prosperũ iter cõtingat uolente deo,

a   ut ueniã

---

23 *Novum Instrumentum*, Basel 1516, Opening of St Paul's Epistles.

NOVVM IN

ſtrumentū omne, diligenter ab ERASMO ROTERODAMO
recognitum & emendatum, nō ſolum ad græcam ueritatem, ue-
tumetiam ad multorum utriuſqʒ linguæ codicum, eorumqʒ ue-
terum ſimul & emendatorum fidem, poſtremo ad pro-
batiſſimorum autorum citationem, emendationem
& interpretationem, præcipue, Origenis, Chry
ſoſtomi, Cyrilli, Vulgarij, Hieronymi, Cy-
priani, Ambroſij, Hilarij, Auguſti-
ni, una cū Annotationibus, quæ
lectorem doceant, quid qua
ratione mutatum ſit.
Quiſquis igitur
amas ue-
ram
Theolo-
giam, lege, cogno
ſce, ac deinde iudica.
Neqʒ ſtatim offendere, ſi
quid mutatum offenderis, ſed
expende, num in melius mutatum ſit.

APVD INCLYTAM
GERMANIAE BASILAEAM.

CVM PRIVILEGIO
MAXIMILIANI CAESARIS AVGVSTI,
NE QVIS ALIVS IN SACRA ROMA-
NI IMPERII DITIONE, INTRA QVATV
OR ANNOS EXCVDAT, AVT ALIBI
EXCVSVM IMPORTET.

24 *Novum Instrumentum*, Basel 1516, Title page.

ment and by experience of his friend, as well as by – as Erasmus expressed it – his penetrating and original intellect, to understand its message. This was the praise of Christian folly, foolishness to the Greeks, the purest contempt for the world and its values in following the commandments of Christ and walking from henceforth in his holy ways, eschewing whatever contaminated gospel ingenuousness. Still more important than the *Folly*, perhaps, the New Testament lies on the shelves, the *Novum Instrumentum*, issued the year before, the first Greek text of the New Testament to be published, though not the first to be printed. The Complutensian Polyglot had been begun earlier and was part ready; but its issue had not been authorized by the Church, and would not be until 1522. The Emperor Maximilian was quicker off the mark to grant the privilege of printing. Froben, with his imitation of a Greek manuscript and his own name in Greek characters, gave it the required style (Fig. 23). The title-page of the *Novum Instrumentum* states the joint humanist credo of More and Erasmus (Fig. 24). The sacred text, it says, has been revised and emended not only by the truth of the Greeks, but also by collation of many manuscripts and by careful consultation of patristic authority. Among those authorities so resoundingly cited, incidentally, is one Vulgarius. This was later to cause embarrassment. Vulgarius never existed. He was really the Byzantine exegete Theophylact, archbishop among the Bulgarians in the late eleventh century, much valued during the Renaissance. William Grocyn's Greek manuscript of him is now in the library of Corpus Christi College, Oxford; and he figures in the library list which I have mentioned above.

Attached to the *Novum Instrumentum* were the *Annotationes*, which grew with successive editions until they had to be accommodated in separate volumes, becoming a theology on their own, and translated into several vernaculars. There was also a Preface, the famous *Paraclesis*, exhorting all, even infidels, Scots, Irish and women, to diligent perusal of the Scriptures. All lovers of true theology, as distinct from the Scholastic variety, the title-page insists, must set themselves to reading, comparing, considering, judging and correcting.

In double column with the *Novum Instrumentum's* Greek is a

25 Jan van Eýck, *St Jerome in his Study*. Detroit, Institute of Arts.

retouched version of the Latin Vulgate of St Jerome, whose works Erasmus had edited in 1516. His supporters had often compared Erasmus to Jerome, and as often Erasmus's opponents had repudiated the comparison. The great four-volume Jerome had been sent to many of Erasmus's English friends, including More, surely, so that it rightly figures from that point of view alone on the shelves. Here Erasmus is without doubt St Jerome, lacking only Jerome's lion. He must have asked to be shown thus, as the greatest of those contemporaries who had chosen the way of sacred scholarship. It is almost as though Massys had taken Jan van Eyck's *St Jerome in his Study* (Fig.25), used what was required for Erasmus in the way of implements and accoutrements, given both the open book and the closed books on the shelves those precise personal references, and redistributed the rest. The sandcaster in van Eyck's *Jerome*, for example, is prominent in the portrait of Gillis, and the jars replaced by Gillis's covered cup.

The *Praise of Folly* and the *Novum Instrumentum* raised a furore. The young Maarten van Dorp of Louvain took it upon himself to remonstrate. He warned Erasmus of the scandal he was causing by his satire and by his insistence on the importance of Greek for New Testament studies, and begged him to make peace with the theologian-logicians by writing a *Praise of Wisdom*. He is aware, he says, of the precedents of Valla and of Jacques Lefèvre d'Etaples. All the same, he goes on, the truth of the matter is that, by concerning oneself with the Greek, one is implying that the Vulgate is in error. This is impossible because, if it were so, God would not have allowed his Church to err for more than a thousand years in accepting it as Gospel. Dorp's position, so vigorously contested at this time by both Erasmus and More, was – it is one of those Reformation ironies – to be embraced by More in his defences of the Church during the 1520s and 1530s. Erasmus replied to Dorp; Dorp replied to Erasmus's reply, reiterating his arguments, without sympathy for Erasmus's position: true religion does not require a knowledge of even the second of the three sacred languages, Greek, let alone of Hebrew, the third. Dorp never goes as far as those later Sorbonne theologians who declare that knowing Greek is liable to make a man a heretic, but he comes close enough. Ironically, within a year or so, the first Collegium Trilingue had been founded at Louvain by Jerome Busleiden, another friend of More's. More replies on behalf of Erasmus, taking Dorp to task, dealing with his invocation of dialectic against the humanists' grammar, Latin and Greek, and comparing Erasmus with Jerome. He would later do this at greater length to the Monk, with a huge accumulation of technical detail. All the objections raised against Erasmus, he was not slow to point out, had been raised by Jerome's opponents against Jerome himself. To Edward Lee, More made the same points.

The printing history of these works has some curious features. The Letter to Dorp, though it formed part of More's Latin *Lucubrationes*, issued at Basel in 1563, did not appear in a separate edition until it was published in 1625 at Leiden. After that, it was printed five times in editions of the *Praise of Folly*, in context as it were. Oddly, it did not appear in print within the lifetime of the controversy to which it had immediate reference, whereas the Letter to a Monk and the Letter to Lee both came out twice in 1520, very topically, and then – suppressed on account perhaps of their Reformation implications – not again until the eighteenth century. Their first appearance in print was entirely typical. Erasmus had them issued as part of the printing programme he orchestrated concerning the extended controversy to which they both had exact reference, a campaign which included Erasmus's own *Apologia de In principio erat sermo*, the celebrated new translation of the first words of St John's Gospel, 'In principio erat verbum', as it sounded in the Vulgate. This had first appeared, not in the *Novum Instrumentum* of 1516, but in the second edition of 1519, more belligerently entitled *Novum Testamentum*. Oddly again, the Letters to a Monk and to Lee did not appear in the Basel edition of 1563, along with the Letter to Dorp which is their natural counterpart.

One has difficulty, then, in fitting the humanistic letters into any context but the immediate one of the controversies of the epoch of their writing, except the rather specious ones of the *Collected Works* and of what may or may not have been a sort of More revival on the Continent and in England during the second quarter of the sixteenth century. The context of these works was one in which More could still proudly ally himself, as a humanist, with the forward-looking side. At about this time he could also proclaim a humanist allegiance through the personal seals which he affixed to documents and letters. One, long known, is the head of the Emperor Titus, a humanist favourite. Titus, the delight and the darling of humankind, as Suetonius calls him, was the Emperor who, when turning over in his mind the events of the day that had passed and finding that he had done no positive good to anyone, was accustomed to say 'My friends, I have lost a day.'

He had also a special place in Renaissance Christian thought as the pagan Emperor who, God's agent unawares, had humbled the pride of the Jews and sacked their city of Jerusalem, as punishment for their antagonism to Christ. Under Titus's head on the seal you can just see, transferred from the reverse of the Roman coin on which the seal, a Renaissance *rifacimento all'antica* is based, the legend IVDAEA CAPTA.[50] At about the same time, More was also using – as we know only since summer 1989 – two other classical seals, this time genuinely antique. The reappearance then of that exciting bundle of 133 letters to Frans van Cranevelt, the Netherlandish humanist friend of so many other humanists, provided us with a new Erasmus autograph, more than thirty letters from Juan Luis Vives, and seven new autograph letters from More, almost doubling the number of undoubted letters in his own hand.[51] Attached to more than one letter of 1521–2 were seals showing Fortuna in a familiar type with patera and cornucopia (Fig. 26). In the same sale at Christie's on 21 June 1989, lot 108 was a deed signed and sealed by More with a bearded male head, perhaps of a Roman

50 J. B. Trapp, 'Thomas More and the visual Arts', *Essays on the Renaissance and the classical Tradition*, Aldershot 1990, viii, pp.38–9; id., 'La iconografía de Santo Tomás Moro', *Lecturas de historia del arte*, ii, 1990, p.50.

51 Christie's, 21 June 1989, lot 91. The bundle has now joined the other two in the library of the Catholic University of Louvain. See *La correspondance Cranevelt*, issued by the Fondation Roi Baudouin, Brussels 1990; H. Schulte Herbrüggen, in *Moreana*, ciii, 1990, pp.49–66; and id., in *Bibliothèque d'humanisme et Renaissance*, lii, 1990, pp.65–76; for this and other seals used by More, see also Trapp, opp. cit. n. 50 above.

26 Seal of Thomas More, 1520–22. Leuven, Katholieke Universiteit, Centrale Bibliotheek.

27 Seal of Thomas More, 1533. Private Collection.

emperor (Fig.27). None of these seals is quite the strong, invariable, personal affirmation of the Terminus device used by Erasmus, with its proud CONCEDO NVLLI. Nevertheless, all three are evidence of More in his capacity as humanist, and his fellowship with Erasmus.

That fellowship remained throughout their joint lives. It was, after all, to Erasmus that More wrote some time between March and June 1533, giving an account of himself and enclosing the text of the epitaph that he had composed for his tomb in Chelsea Old Church.[52] Among other self-revelations, the epitaph proclaimed its author to have been – in the words of its translation in More's *English Works* of 1557 – 'to theves, murderers and heretikes greuous', as indeed his oath of office as Lord Chancellor had required him to be. Moreover, before taking up that office, he had promised his friend and bishop, Cuthbert Tunstal, who is also mentioned in the epitaph, that he would deal with heresy in print as faithfully as in him lay. His retort upon Tyndale's remark about his darling Erasmus, however tortuous

52 Erasmus, Letter 2831; Allen, x, pp.260–1; *'King's good Servant'*, no. 287.

its syntax, is a measure of the man who knew where the lines had been drawn after the revolt of Luther:

> I say therefore in these days in which men by their own default misconstrue and take harm of the very scripture of God, until men better amend, if any man would now translate *Moria* into English, or some works either that I have written ere this, albeit there be no harm therein, folk yet being, as they be, given to take harm of that that is good, I would not only my darling's books but mine own also, help to burn them with mine own hands, rather than that folk should, though through their own fault, take any harm of them, seeing that I see them likely in these days so to do.[53]

Erasmus's New Testament studies presented a considerable problem for More. Erasmus's replacement, in his new translation of the New Testament, of the hallowed words of the Latin Vulgate, 'sermo' for 'verbum' for example, had prompted More to defend his friend in published works and in disputation at court. This was very well; debate was in a learned language and the problem of understanding in a sense derogatory to true religion was well in the background, except to the most died-in-the-wool conservative, concerned for total consensus. On the other hand, matters did not cease there. Erasmus had sometimes used the word 'congregatio' for the Vulgate's 'ecclesia', church. This usage both excised a whole dimension and added a desperately new one. The Church was more than the congregation, the body of present-day believers; it was also the everlastingly God-guided repository of truth and tradition. This was very well for the stateless, scholarly Erasmus, but for those who had the peace of a realm at heart and the participation of that realm in what More called 'the common corps of Christendom', there was danger of what he also called 'misorder and abusion'. 'Congregatio', Luther's *Gemeinde*, and Tyndale's 'congregation', lent itself easily to the notion of the priesthood of all believers, so that individual, separatist belief was set up against the weight of the ages and the validation of the Holy Ghost.

Similarly, when Tyndale told the world that the Church had

---

53 *Confutation of Tyndale's Answer*, ii, London and New Haven, 1973 = Yale Edition viii, p.179.

a conspiracy to prevent laymen from reading Scripture and that this was

> not for the love of your souls (which they care for as the fox doth for the geese) . . . insomuch as they permit and suffer you to read Robin Hood, and Bevis of Hampton, Hercules, Hector and Troilus . . . ribaldry, as filthy as heart can think,[54]

there was mortal danger. When Tyndale remedied the situation by following Luther's example in making a vernacular translation of the New Testament, and when that translation began to circulate illicitly in England, More could see only a malicious mind in the renderings that Tyndale adopted and, like the experienced prosecuting counsel that he was, he endlessly establishes and emphasizes *mens rea*. Another of these translations that More found deliberately misleading was the word 'senior', a literal translation from the Greek, for the orthodox 'priest', confirming that Tyndale was lewd Luther's ape in attacking the sacraments of the Church. Thus to set aside the sacrament of orders could only seem to More to bespeak the presence of a vicious intent to corrupt the easily corruptible people and to send their souls to hell. Worse still was Tyndale's use of 'love' for *caritas*, which struck not only at the works of mercy, at the notion of merit co-operating with grace, but at the central doctrine of Christian, holy love, of *agape*. The usage obliterated the vital distinction between this sacred sentiment and, as More put it, 'the lewd love that is between Fleck and his mate.' Luther had shown his indifference to another sacrament besides orders: in marrying his nun, Katharina von Bora, he had violated the sacrament of marriage as well. More belabours him unmercifully and often obscenely, for this breaking of a vow, an oath – which was always for him, until the last, a matter of the highest importance.[55]

54 William Tyndale, *Obedience of a Christian Man*, Preface, in id., *Doctrinal Treatises*, Parker Society, i, Cambridge 1848, p.160.
55 On tendentious translation, see More, *Dialogue concerning Heresies*, New Haven and London 1981 = Yale Edition, vi, pp.285–90; *Confutation of Tyndale's Answer*, New Haven and London 1973 = Yale Edition, viii, pp.143–5 etc. (see Index).

III

Erasmus, John Colet, Thomas More and Thomas Linacre

THE EXCURSION into religious opinion and the vernacular at the end of my second lecture took me some distance from the English humanists of my title and their books. On the other hand, I did not desert the New Testament, that prime document of evangelical humanism, so that I need only consider four large manuscripts containing the Epistles, Gospels, Acts and Revelation, in Latin, to be firmly back on the rails. The reason for the curious order in which I name the New Testament books will appear shortly.

In 1504, after his discovery of Valla's *Annotationes in Novum Testamentum* and his publication of that compendium of *philosophia Christi*, his *Enchiridion militis Christiani, Manual of the Christian Soldier*, Erasmus set himself in earnest to the New Testament and its text, improving his Greek in order to do so. He also appealed to Colet for help, and in 1505 came to London, as he had asked Colet if he might do, relying on Colet's goodwill and assistance. Colet had not long become Dean of St Paul's. In October, his father Sir Henry Colet, Mercer and twice Mayor of London, having died, John came into the patrimony which he was later to use to found St Paul's School. Even after

■mnipotenti, Jnuifibili, Jncomprehenfibili, trino, vniqʒ deo: Chrifhferi virgi
ni Marie Speciofiffime: totri quoqʒ celorum exercitui, fit laus honor
atqʒ victoria: quorum ope & adiutorio prefens confcriptus eſt
liber, fumpribus atqʒ expenfis Keuerendi Domini Joannis
Colet Diui Pauli ecclefie Londini Decani, ac Sacre Theolo
gie profefforis eximii: Egregii viri Henrici Colet
Equitis aurati, opulentiffime Ciuitatis Londini Se
natoris, atqʒ eiufdem bis Confulis, filii: arte vero atqʒ induftria Petri
Meghen Monoculi, Teutonis natione Brabantini, Oppidi Bufchiducefi, Leo
dieri Dioces. Anno dominice Jncarnationis Millimoʟiungentefimo
Sexto Kl Nouembris: Regm vero
Jnuictiffimi Principis ac Sereniffimi Re
gis Anglie Henrici Septimi vigefimofedo.

■odem anno Nobiliffimus Princeps Jlluftriffimufqʒ Philippus Rex Ca
ftilie Argonie & Archidux Auftrie Dux Burgonie Brabantie & tempe
ftate compellente in Angliam applicuit. Quem Strenuiffimus Rex
Henricus vii.ᵒ fupradi
ctus, vt pater fili
um recepit: fu
ma humanitate tractauit, maximis honoribus de
corauit, plurimis muneribus dotauit. Qui
k Octobris viam vniuerfe carnis ingreffus eſt.
Cuius anime ac
omniü fideliü de
functoꝗ mifereri
dignetur
altiffimus
Amai.

28 British Library, Royal MS I E.V, vol.ii, fol. 358v.

provision for Dame Christian, Sir Henry's widow who outlived her only surviving son by three years, to die in 1522, John was a wealthy man both in his own right and from his church stipends and benefices. Colet encouraged Erasmus, lent him some manuscripts and promised him others. In return, he received no Lucian dedication from Erasmus, who probably judged rightly in thinking Lucian too indirect and frivolous for Colet's taste. He must surely have remembered how Colet had taken at face value the rhetorical dispraise of classical learning intended for the second book of the *Antibarbari*. All the same, it is a little surprising, given that the similarly pious Richard Whitford, translator of the *Imitation of Christ*, was accorded one, along with Fox, Ruthall and Urswick, those influential clerics from whom, along with William Warham, by then Archbishop of Canterbury, Erasmus was building his circle of English patrons.

This second visit by Erasmus to England was not protracted. He was back in France at the beginning of June 1506, about the time that Colet must have commissioned Pieter Meghen to write, and to have decorated with a frontispiece in the fashionable Ghent–Bruges style, an imposing manuscript of the Pauline and Catholic Epistles. This is now one of two volumes under the pressmark Royal MS 1 E. V in the British Library. Its colophon indicates that it was completed on 1 November and that, like later volumes, it was intended in some sense as a memorial to Sir Henry (Fig. 28). It was an affirmation also, in its content, of Colet's reverence for St Paul, which had earlier found expression in the famous lectures on I Corinthians and on Romans that Colet had delivered in Oxford from the 1490s. Three years later, in 1509, on 8 May and 7 September respectively, Meghen completed companion volumes, each with frontispieces and each with a similar colophon, containing Matthew and Mark and Luke and John. Luke and John form the other component of Royal MS 1 E. V in the British Library; Matthew and Mark are in Cambridge University Library.

The frontispieces to the Pauline Epistles (Fig. 29) and to Matthew and Mark (Fig. 30) are of distinctly superior quality to those of Luke and John. All are in an accomplished version,

AVLVS
SERVS

Liber Epła Diui Pauli Apłi:

Epiſtola Diui Pauli ad Romanos:

29 British Library, Royal MS I E. V, vol. ii, fol. 5.

nevertheless, of the style described by John Skelton in *The Garland of Laurel*:

> With that, of the boke losende were the claspis.
> The margent was illumynid all with golden railles
> And byse, enpicturid with gressoppis and waspis,
> With butterflyis and fresse pecoke taylis,
> Enflorid with flowris and slymy snaylis,
> Envyvid picturis well towchid and quikly.
> It wolde have made a man whole that had be ryght sekely . . .

Skelton's description of Occupation's book, which the Queen of Fame has commanded to be opened in order to see whether the name of John Skelton, *poeta laureatus*, is enshrined in it is, as far as I know, unique as a contemporary description of the style that was still very much in English vogue when Skelton began to put together the *Garland* – that is to say in the mid-1490s – and which retained its position, both as native Netherlandish work and as English imitation of it, almost to the end of the reign of Henry VIII. How prevalent the taste was is shown, for instance, in the border that was sometimes used by John Rastell to frame his printer's mark (Fig.31). This vignette, with its Last Judgment atop the four concentric spheres of the elements earth, water, air and fire, is a good example of how many printers' woodcut blocks go back to manuscript models not merely of the fifteenth century, but ultimately of the twelfth and thirteenth. In this case one has a poor-relation descendant of one of the elaborate frontispieces to the sumptuous manuscripts of the *Bible moralisée*. Rastell's elaborate device is flanked by a crude black-and-white woodcut version of one of those animated and colourful Ghent-Bruges borders. There could hardly be a better example of currency.[1]

In the New Testament manuscripts of London and Cambridge, Erasmus's new Latin version is written into the narrower of two columns. Erasmus had caused scandal by omitting

---

1 The example illustrated is from Rastell's *Statuta in parliamento* of perhaps 1530; see also the border framing the title-page woodcut of John Skelton's *Dyuers Balettys*, printed by Rastell about 1527 (Fig. 13 above).

Mattli,m. A.　Nicium euange. A.　Nitium
euange.
lii IESV Chrish filii dei (ficut　lii IESV Chrish
filii dei, sicut
fcriptum eft in ESaia propheta　fcriptum eft in
prophetis.
Ecce ego mitto
Malach, m.A　Ecce mitto angelum meum an　nunciū meum
ante faciem tuā
te faciem tuam: qui preparabit　qui preparabit

30 Cambridge University Library, MS Dd.vii.3, fol.180.

31 John Rastell, *Statuta in Parliamento*, ?1530.

from the *Novum Instrumentum* in 1516, both in the Greek and therefore from the Latin, the famous proof-text for the Trinity in I John, concerning the three witnesses in heaven, the so-called *comma Johanneum*. The Trinity is not referred to anywhere else in Scripture. The *comma*, Erasmus argued, was in no text drawn straight from the fountain-head, from the Greek. It must therefore be a later interpolation. He was, of course, correct, but he added that, if a Greek text could be produced that contained the *comma*, he would put it back for the next printing. Two manuscripts were promptly produced, one of them so promptly as to make Erasmus say that it had been written especially to confute him. Nevertheless, in the *Novum Testamentum* of 1519, the *comma* duly reappeared. And there it is, in both the Vulgate and the Erasmus text of the manuscript written for Colet. In 1516 also, however, Erasmus had been less radical in most of his retouching of the Vulgate. The reading of John I.1 there is still 'In principio erat verbum.' In Colet's manuscript the reading is 'In principio erat sermo' (Fig.32). So here is a puzzle. Colet's manuscript contains an Erasmus version that is both less bold than and equally as bold as the first printed edition. P. S. Allen had warned that the Erasmus text conformed roughly to one of the later printings of Erasmus's Latin. It was known that Meghen transcribed his manuscripts almost exclusively from printed books. The cataloguers of the Royal manuscripts remarked cautiously that space had been left in Colet's manuscripts for a commentary, as had been done in the Gallican Psalter, now MS 1 E. III among those same manuscripts (Figs. 33–34). The Psalter's commentary space has, in fact, been filled by Meghen (I believe), using two different hands, a sort of formal, upright cross between roman and italic, and cursive italic, with a commentary the authorship of which I have not been able to discover. All this should have been a warning against hasty hypothesis. On the other hand, there were exceptions to the rule about Meghen's transcriptions being from printed books, and those exceptions were precisely transcriptions of Colet's manuscripts. So hasty hypothesis had its way. Erasmus, one decided, was willing to go much farther, be more radical, for Colet in private than he was to be for the public in 1516. We had, as Erwin Panofsky used to say, nothing to fear but the facts. Andrew Brown's painstaking study both of the chronology of Erasmus's dealings with the New Testament text and of Pieter Meghen's hand has provided us with the truth. The Erasmus version was indeed written into space left for commentary in Colet's manuscripts, and it was written in after Colet's death, when the manuscripts had passed into other ownership.[2]

2 Andrew J. Brown, 'The Date of Erasmus' Latin Translation of the New Testament', *Transactions of the Cambridge Bibliographical Society*, viii,4, 1984, pp.351–80.

N principio erat
sermo, et sermo .A. erat verbum, et verbum erat a
erat apud deum,
et deus erat ille pud deum, et deus erat verbū.
sermo. Hic erat
in principio apud Hoc erat in principio apud de
deum. Omnia per
ipfum facta sūt: um. Omnia per ipm facta
et sine eo factum
eft nihil, quod fa funt: et sine ipo factum eft
ctum eft.
In ipfo vita erat, nihil. Quod factum eft in ip
et vita erat lux
hominū, fo vita erat: et vita erat lux
et lux in tene
bris lucet, hominū et lux in tenebris lu
et tenebre eam
non apprehen cet: et tenebre eam non com
derunt.

prehenderunt.

Erat homo miffus
a deo, cui no Fuit homo miffus a deo cui
men Ioannes.

nomen erat Joannes. Hic ve

Matth. iii. A
Marci. i. A

Dirumpamus vincula eorum:

& proiciamus a nobis iugum ipsorum.

Qui habitat in celis irridebit eos:

& dominus subsannabit eos.

Tunc loquetur ad eos in ira sua:

& in furore suo conturbabit eos.

Ego autem constitutus sum rex ab eo:

sup[er] syon montem s[an]c[tu]m eius, p[re]dicans p[re]ceptu[m] eius.

D[omi]n[u]s dixit ad me filius meus es tu:

ego hodie genui te.

Postula a me,

& dabo tibi gentes hereditatem tua[m]:

Quid est domine q̃ tu quum sis creaturarum omnium opifex &
moderator, me tuis obsequijs addictum sinas ab eis infestari

Siue pungant creaturæ siue blandiantur
semper pias mentes inquietant

In tribulantes. Mundus cũ his q̃ in mũdo
sunt

In insurgentes. Caro cũ vitijs & corrupsce-
tijs

& deijcentes. Satanas cũ satellitio suo

Ne qd multiplicati sunt q̃ tribulant me:

Quid est insuper q̃ tot vitiosæ atq̃ prauorum affectuum rebello;
nem in carne mea sustineant

multi insurgunt aduersum me.

Prauoq̃ affectuũ aduersus aĩm insurrectio
Reluctationem carnis contra spm̃ indicat

Quid est præterea q̃ tot maligni spiritus animæ insidiantur
meæ suggerentes, vt alibi q̃ apud te salutem queram

ulti dicunt anime mee:

Vbi tandem a mundo carneq̃ superati sum?
desperationem nobis demones ingerunt

Et quasi tu nullam de me solicitudinem haberes, dissuadent
quicquam abs te sperare subsidij

non est salus ipsi in deo eius.

Primum ideo fit, vt quoties periculum immineat, ad te con/
fugiam qui me non illibenter suscipies

tribulantes ─┐
             ├ susceptor
insurgentes ─┤ Deus Gloria
             │
deijcentes ──┴ Exaltans caput

Tu autem dñe susceptor meus es:

Et contra maculas & neuos quibus ab impuris carnis affec/
tibus animus inquinatur de tua purgatione glorier

Quomodo mater in sinum recipit filium
& brachijs ac manibus eum operit

gloria mea,

De quo soli gloriemur non de viribus ñris

Et quantum animam meam deijcere spiritus impij moliuntur
tu contra tantum spe firma tuæ benignitatis subleuare conaris

& exaltans caput meum.

Subleuans mentem spirituali solamine

Magno cordis desiderio quod in auribus dei strepitum
ingentem facit vociferatus sum

Uoce mea ad dominũ clamaui:

Desiderium vehemens cordis, clamor est
in auribus dei

Et ille sine mora de summo cœlorum fastigio dignatus
fuit votis fauere meis

& exaudiuit me de monte sancto suo.

Ego partim foris a creaturis, partim intus ab affectibus carnis
in profundum peccati somnum actus sum. Et suauis admodũ
illa soporatio mihi visa est, oblectauitq̃ me vehementer

Somno peccati dormit qui lapsus in peccata
Soporatur q̃ somno immergitur & eum somnũ
vehementer dulcis est

sperantem ─┐
           ├ exaudit
piscentem ─┤ Deus suscipit
           │
fidentem ──┴ subleuat

Ego dormiui & soporatus sum:

Ego tamen resipui tandem, excussaq̃ grauedine soporationis illiꝰ que
me sic blanditer oppressit. Ves id nullis meis viribus effectum
est sed tuis optime deus q̃ me sic excitasti, vt sis ipse solꝰ meæ gloria

Exurgere a somno resipiscere a peccato

& exurrexi, qa dñs suscepit me.

Si mihi demonum myriades obiecerint non esse abs
te salutem haud concidam animo

Non timebo milia ppli circundantis me,

34 British Library, Royal MS 1 E.III, fol. 3.

When then, and why were the transcriptions of Erasmus's text made? Colet's will contains the following clause:

> . . . the New Testament, and oder of myne own making wrytin in parchement, as Coments on Paulis Epesteles and Abbreviacions with many such, I will shall be dispossed at the disposicion of myn executours whiche disposicion I leue to their discrecion and all my bokes imprynted in paper I will also by them be disposed to poore studentes and especially to suche as hathe bene schollers with me . . .

His bequests also included, one might mention in passing:

> . . . to Maister John Bambrughe a silver pott . . . my bed at Charterhous [in Sheen] that I lay upon my self with matresse and blanketts, to the said bed belonging, and certeine of my prynted books called seint Jerom works [surely Erasmus's edition], and other that may be conveniently gyuen vnto hym . . .[3]

So where did those parchments go? Some of them, it seems, to St Paul's School. Colet's widowed mother was one of his executors, and may have felt this fitting. Were the rest, the New Testament manuscripts, thought fit for a King? If so, when did they enter the royal collection, where two of them at least still are? And when was Erasmus's version written in? And when did one volume migrate to Cambridge? And when, finally, was the splendid, more sumptuous, infinitely finer manuscript of Acts and Revelation now at Hatfield House written by Meghen and decorated by one of the Horenbouts? The Hatfield manuscript's curious combination of New Testament books, found nowhere else, as far as I am aware, but completing the tally of books if added to Colet's volumes, indicates that it was intended to make up the set. All of it, the Vulgate and the Erasmus versions both, is written in Meghen's later hand, the hand in which the Erasmus version is written into Colet's manuscripts. It was

---

3 Colet's will is printed in S. Knight, *Life of Colet,* 1724, ed. London 1823, pp.400–9.

Rimū quidē .A. Vperiore quidem
sermonem fe volumine dixi

35 Hatfield House, Cecil Papers MS 324, fol. 1.

clearly intended for Henry and Katherine of Aragon, since it shows their initials bound by true love knots, and their badges (Fig. 35). It must surely belong to the late 1520s, if not the 1530s, before the King's estrangement from Katherine could be publicly proclaimed. Perhaps from the time when Meghen was bidding to become Writer of the King's Books, the position he held from 1530 until his death in 1540. When and how did Burghley, as one assumes, get hold of it? We know that he owned at least one other of Colet's writings in Meghen's manuscript, the fair copy of the ps-Dionysius *Abbreviations*, now Additional MS 63853 in the British Library (Fig. 36). Was this a manifestation of real intellectual interest? And did Cambridge owe its volume of the Colet's New Testament ultimately to Burghley or to Matthew Parker?

To all these questions, I am sorry to say, I have no firm answer. One would like also to know more about that elaborate manuscript of the whole New Testament, the Vulgate text and Erasmus's translation in alternate black and red lines, two volumes, in a smaller format than the Royal manuscripts, now in Corpus Christi College, Oxford (Fig. 37). They were made for an unknown patron, probably in the 1520s. Again, they were written by Pieter Meghen, in his later script. Surely, there were few men in England who had the means to commission an object of such luxury and sumptuousness, with its beautifully elaborate small initials, and its miniatures based on current engravings. The portrait of St Mark, for example, at the head of his Gospel, is founded on Albrecht Dürer's engraving of St Jerome in his study of 1514. Was it a commission from the King? The King had such a thing already, it seems. Would he have wanted another set? Or Cardinal Wolsey? Wolsey would surely have been the only other man in England with the taste to want such a splendid codex, and the resources to commission it. He is a likely enough candidate, especially in view of the magnificent evangeliary and lectionary that he commissioned about 1528 from Meghen, to be decorated by a Horenbout for use in Cardinal College. One of these manuscripts is now in Christ Church, the other in Magdalen College, Oxford. Their miniatures, as Sheila Hardie has shown, are heavily dependent on the

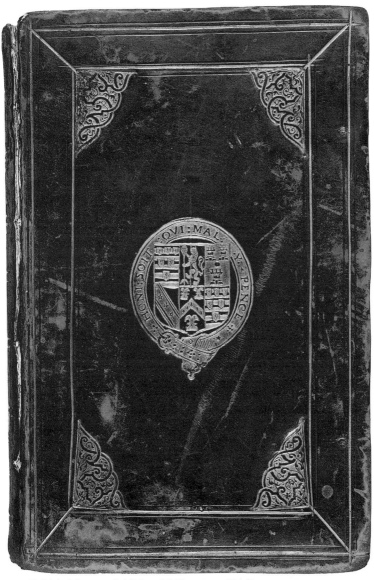

36 British Library, Additional MS 63853. Binding.

Nitiū euangelii Iesu
Christi filii dei sicut
scriptū est in Esaia p
pheta Ecce mitto an
gelum meū ante fa
ciem tuā: qui prepa
rabit viam tuā ante
te. Vox clamantis in
deserto. Parate viam domini: rectas facite semitas eius.
Fuit in deserto Ioannes baptizans et predicans baptis
mū penitentie in remissionē peccatorū. Et egrediebatur
ad eū omnis Iudee regio, et Hierosolymite vniuersi:
et baptizabantur ab illo in Iordanis flumine, confiten
tes peccata sua. Et erat Ioannes vestitus pilis cameloҳ,
et zona pellicea circa lumbos eius, et locustas et mel
siluestre edebat: et predicabat dicens. Venit fortior

37 Oxford, Corpus Christi College, MS 13, fol.68.

Galeni de sanitate tuenda Libri sex Thoma Linacro Anglo Interprete.

38 Galen, *De sanitate tuenda*, translated Thomas Linacre, Paris 1517, Title-page.

prints of Dürer, in particular the Passions and the Life of the Virgin.[4] For Wolsey also, Meghen wrote yet another manuscript, the small, pink and pretty list of the Bishops of Winchester, among whom Wolsey just managed to be and which he may have had bound in the Low Countries or in England, since the stamps on the binding were used in both countries.[5]

Neither Wolsey's taste for the sumptuous nor Henry's appetite for objects needs emphasis. Nevertheless, the presentation copies to each of them of Thomas Linacre's new translations of Galen from Greek into Latin, landmarks in Tudor humanism, would make the point. They are on vellum, with elaborately embellished title-pages and manuscript dedications.[6] Linacre's version of Galen's *De sanitate tuenda* was printed at Paris by Guillaume Le Rouge in 1517 (Fig. 38). The title-page of Wolsey's copy has been enhanced with colour, and there is a manuscript dedication in Linacre's elegant italic autograph. The title-page shows Wolsey's arms, the English royal arms, Galen and Linacre in the spandrels of the architectural title-page above; and Mars and Venus presiding in the flanks, as those for whose service health is worth preserving. Its binding, of concentric rows of arabesque tools and fleurs-de-lis, gilt and decorated in blue, has been attributed to the same French workshop as was employed for the dedication copies of Linacre's *Methodus medendi*. Like the other copies of Galen presented to Henry and to Wolsey, this one found its way into the old Royal Library, and bears its pressmark. Though the translation itself is dedicated to Henry, his copy is no longer extant.

Wolsey's copy of Linacre's translation of Galen's *Methodus medendi*, also on vellum, is also elaborately decorated, though Wolsey's arms were never coloured in. Like the *De sanitate*

---

4 M.Phil. thesis, University of Bristol, 1984.

5 Oxford, Bodleian Library, MS. Rawlinson C.779; cf. J. B. Trapp, 'Notes on MSS written by Peter Meghen', *Book Collector*, xxiv,1, 1975, p.92, no. 16; and, additionally for the binding stamps, *5 Jaar Aanwinsten 1969–73. Tentoonstelling . . . Koninklijke Bibliothek*, Brussels 1975, HSS. no. 59.

6 Giles Barber, 'Thomas Linacre: A bibliographical Survey of his Works', *Linacre Studies. Essays on the Life and Works of Thomas Linacre, c.1460–1524*, ed. F. Maddison, M. Pelling and C. Webster, Oxford 1977, esp.pp.296–9.

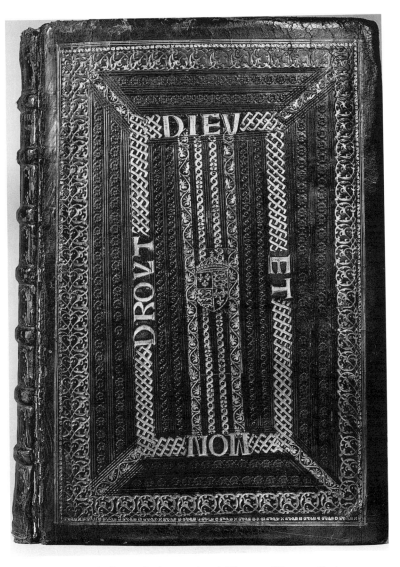

39 Galen, *Methodus medendi*, translated Thomas Linacre, Paris 1519, Binding.

tuenda, it has an elaborate manuscript dedication. Again, it is a Paris printing, this time by Désiré Mahieu, of 1519. Henry's vellum copy, which has survived, is still more lavishly garnished, and has a fine contemporary Parisian binding (Fig. 39), from the atelier of Simon Vostre, with the royal arms and the motto DIEU ET MON DROIT.[7]

Linacre had become royal tutor as well as Greek mentor to Thomas More on his return from study in Italy in 1499 and assistance in Venice to Aldus Manutius with the *editio princeps* of Aristotle in Greek (Fig. 40).[8] Erasmus's annotated copy is extant, one volume of it in King's College, Cambridge, the others in the Library of Wells Cathedral. Linacre was the only native Englishman of the group with whom I am concerned to have attained contemporary Italian humanist standards. In Florence he had been the student of Demetrius Chalcondyles and Angelo Poliziano in Greek, together with the Williams, Grocyn and Latimer, and Giovanni de' Medici, the future Pope Leo X. As one can see from his books and manuscripts, he had learned to write an elegant humanist hand in Latin and in Greek, and to turn an elaborate compliment, recommending to Wolsey, for example, both himself and the thirteen-hundred-year-tried precepts for male health offered by Galen. Linacre had translated ps-Proclus *On the Sphere*. Since 1509 he had been royal physician. Clearly, these fine presentation copies were made with thanks for past favours and a lively sense of future ones – personal, certainly, but also perhaps for the Royal College of Physicians, effectively founded in 1518.

Presentation copies of others of Linacre's works are extant. Richard Fox's copy of *De sanitate tuenda*, with manuscript dedication, is in the Library of the Royal College of Physicians; and a vellum copy of the *De temperamentis*, which perhaps once belonged to Cuthbert Tunstal, is in the Bodleian. The *De temperamentis* was printed at Cambridge by John Siberch; the presentation binding on the Bodleian copy uses the same panel-stamps as were used in the same year by the London stationer

7 G. Barber, loc. cit.
8 C. B. Schmitt, in *Contemporaries of Erasmus*, ii, Toronto 1986, pp. 331–2.

ἔμψυχον ἀπέβλεψαν, ὅπερ τὸ κινητικώτατον ὑπέλαβον τῇ ψυ
χῇ. ὅσοι δ᾽ ἐπὶ τὸ γινώσκειν ᾗ καὶ αἰσθάνεσθαι τῶν ὄντων, οὗτοι δὲ λέ
γουσι τὴν ψυχὴν τὰς ἀρχάς. οἱ μὲν πλείους ποιοῦντες ταύτας ἐρ
γάζονται οἱ δὲ μίαν ταύτην, ὥσπερ Ἐμπεδοκλῆς μὲν ἐκ τῶν στοι
χείων πάντων. εἶναι δὲ καὶ ἕκαστον ψυχὴν τούτων οὕτω λέγων.
Γαίῃ μὲν γὰρ γαῖαν ὀπώπαμεν, ὕδατι δ᾽ ὕδωρ. αἰθέρι δ᾽ αἰθέ-
ρα δῖον. ἀτὰρ πυρὶ πῦρ ἀΐδηλον. στοργῇ δὲ στοργήν. νεῖκος δὲ
τε νείκεϊ λυγρῷ. τὸν αὐτὸν δὲ τρόπον ἐν τῷ Τιμαίῳ Πλάτων τὴν
ψυχὴν ἐκ τῶν στοιχείων ποιεῖ. γινώσκεσθαι γὰρ ὁμοίῳ ὅμοιον.
τὰ δὲ πράγματα τὰ ἐκ τῶν ἀρχῶν εἶναι. ὁμοίως δὲ καὶ ἐν τοῖς
περὶ φιλοσοφίαν λεγομένοις διωρίσθη. αὐτὸ μὲν τὸ ζῷον ἐκ τῆς τοῦ
ἑνὸς ἰδέας καὶ τοῦ πρώτου μήκους καὶ πλάτους καὶ βάθους. τὰ
δ᾽ ἄλλα ὁμοιοτρόπως. Ἔτι δὲ καὶ ἄλλως. νοῦν μὲν τὸ ἓν ἐπιστήμην
δὲ τὰ δύο. μοναχῶς γὰρ ἐφ᾽ ἓν τὸν ἀριθμὸν. τὸν δὲ τοῦ ἐπιπέδου, δόξαν.
αἴσθησιν δὲ τὸν τοῦ στερεοῦ. οἱ μὲν γὰρ ἀριθμοὶ, τὰ εἴδη αὐτὰ καὶ αἱ ἀρχαὶ
ἐλέχθησαν. εἰσὶ δὲ ἐκ τῶν στοιχείων. κρίνεται δὲ τὰ πράγματα τὰ μὲν νῷ. τὰ δ᾽ ἐπιστήμῃ. τὰ δὲ δόξῃ, τὰ δ᾽ αἰσθήσει. εἴδη δ᾽ οἱ
ἀριθμοὶ οὗτοι τῶν πραγμάτων. ἐπεὶ δὲ καὶ κινητικὸν ἐδόκει ἡ ψυ
χὴ εἶναι καὶ γνωριστικὸν, οὕτως ἔνιοι συνέπλεξαν ἐξ ἀμφοῖν. ἀ
ποφηνάμενοι τὴν ψυχὴν ἀριθμὸν κινοῦνθ᾽ ἑαυτόν. διαφέρονται
δὲ περὶ τῶν ἀρχῶν τίνες καὶ πόσαι. μάλιστα μὲν οἱ σωματικὰς ποι
οῦντες τὰς ἀσωμάτους. τούτοις δ᾽ οἱ μίξαντες καὶ ἀπ᾽ ἀμφοῖν τὰς
ἀρχὰς ἀποφηνάμενοι. διαφέρονται δὲ καὶ περὶ τὸ πλῆθος. οἱ
μὲν γὰρ μίαν. οἱ δὲ πλείους λέγουσιν. ἑπομένως δὲ τούτοις.
καὶ τὴν ψυχὴν ἀποδιδόασι. τό τε γὰρ κινητικὸν τὴν φύσιν τῶν
πρώτων ὑπειλήφασιν οὐκ ἀλόγως. ὅθεν ἔδοξέ τισι πῦρ εἶναι. καὶ γὰρ τοῦτο λεπτομερέστατόν τε. καὶ μάλιστα τῶν στοιχείων
ἀσώματον, ἔτι τε κινεῖταί τε καὶ κινεῖ τὰ ἄλλα πρώτως. Δημό-
κριτος δὲ καὶ γλαφυρωτέρως εἴρηκεν ἀποφαινόμενος, διὰ
τί τούτων ἑκάτερον. ψυχὴν μὲν γὰρ εἶναι ταὐτὸ καὶ νοῦν.

40 Aristotle, *Opera omnia*, Venice 1495–8, vol.iii, with notes by
Erasmus.

John Raynes for the eleven surviving presentation copies of Henry VIII's *Assertio septem sacramentorum*.

Besides being a physician, Linacre was preoccupied with more narrowly humanist matters, in particular Latin grammar.[9] The story of how he was requested by John Colet to write a Latin grammar for use in St Paul's School and how the result was rejected as too advanced for tender minds, is well known, if not entirely clear as to detail. No-one could ever have accused Colet of not being clear and downright in his views, or of not knowing what he wanted and did not want. When we come to attempt to assess his reading and his library, however, we are continually brought up short for lack of information.

Thanks to Colet's conveyance to the Mercers and to other documents, including the will of 1514 in the Court of Hustings, we have a fairly full knowledge of his real property. There is, however, no inventory of his chattels and his books. As we have seen above, his last will made a number of specific bequests of money, plate and other objects.[10] The images on the walls of his lodgings in the Charterhouse at Sheen get special mention, rather unusually for the will of someone in that middle-high position in the ecclesiastical hierarchy: like all 'bordwork' there, they are to remain perpetually *in situ*. We have seen how he disposed of some of his books, manuscript and other. Additionally, Henry Digby is left a treasured book of devotion: 'my lytell prymer coverd with green velvet'. 'Thomas Lupeshed my schollar' is to 'be rememberd after the discreccion of myn executors and to haue all suche bookes prynted as may be most necessary for his lernyng', while all Colet's 'bokes imprynted in paper' are to be 'disposed to poore studentes and especially to suche as hath bene schollers with me', at the discretion of his executors. His copy of Erasmus's Jerome, we have seen, was specially bestowed. Of others, his 'New Testament' which, one

---

9 D. F. S. Thomson, 'Linacre's Latin Grammars', *Linacre Studies*, pp.24–35; K. Jensen, '*De emendata structura latini sermonis*: The Latin Grammar of Thomas Linacre', *Journal of the Warburg and Courtauld Institutes*, xlix, 1986, pp.106–25.

10 Above, p.90.

supposes, could have been his manuscript versions or the printed *Novum Instrumentum/Testamentum,* or both, and 'other of my own writing in parchment, as Coments on Paulis Epesteles and Abbreviacions with many such other', Colet left the bestowal to his executors. Some may have gone to St Paul's School – and left it soon after, perhaps. Just as well, if so: it looks as if much, if not all, of the School library may have perished in the Great Fire. The very late list, printed by Samuel Knight, of the School library is little help.[11] It is full of seventeenth- and even eighteenth-century books. The appearance in it of an occasional incunable Horace, Terence or Cicero, or Johannes Trithemius's *Catalogus illustrium virorum,* or Niccolò Perotti's *Cornucopia,* or an Aldine Aulus Gellius – an author whom Thomas More relished[12] – or the Greek bucolic poets, all in editions printed in Colet's lifetime, is therefore uninformative.

I have suggested above a way for Colet's New Testament manuscripts to have entered the Royal collection. By what intermediaries others of his manuscripts and the one printed book that we know to have survived from his library reached their sixteenth-century locations, where these are known, let alone the places where they have subsequently been preserved, is too often a mystery. It would be good if one could somehow connect with Colet that large and handsome glossed Gallican Psalter, written by Meghen, now Royal MS 1 E. III, but the mere indication in it of topics arranged in triplicities, according to Colet's inclination as recorded by Erasmus, is hardly enough.

Can another and finer codex among the Royal manuscripts, insufficiently studied, also perhaps be connected with Colet (Fig. 41)? There is no sign of him anywhere in it, however. Royal MS 1 D. XI–XV was transcribed by Pieter Meghen, using his earlier hand, which Andrew Brown has shown to change at 1517 or thereabouts.[13] It carries the old royal pressmark, no. 1264, written on the flyleaf after the name 'petrus monoculus'. It is

11 *Life of Colet,* Oxford 1823, pp.409–26.
12 R. J. Schoeck, 'More's Attic Nights: Sir Thomas More's Use of Aulus Gellius' *Noctes Atticae', Renaissance News,* xiii, 1960, pp.127–29.
13 Brown, art. cit. n. 2 above.

41 British Library, Royal MS 1 D.XI–XV, vol.i, fols.91v–92.

just possible that this is the scribe's autograph signature. The manuscript itself is of the Pauline Epistles, but the basis of the text is not the Vulgate, nor is it any of Erasmus's versions. What we have is another version altogether, written in black with the Vulgate readings carefully recorded in red where they differ from the main text. This is not done in double columns or in alternate red and black lines, but the variants are elaborately interposed. So scrupulously is this done that the ink will sometimes be changed within a word. Where the new translation reads 'sonum' for example, and the Vulgate 'sonitum', 'son-'

is in black, '-it-' in red, and '-um' again in black; or the word 'contemptabilia' will be divided, after its third syllable, between black and red according to the two texts. There are slips and omissions, but the whole gives an impression of care and tidiness. As well as the Vulgate, there is another less frequent source of variants, which I have not succeeded in identifying. It went unnoticed by the cataloguers of the Royal manuscripts. Its readings are recorded in purple. Their origin is not Erasmus's *Novum Instrumentum* and on palaeographical grounds it cannot be one of the later editions of Erasmus's translation. It is not the *Annotationes* of Valla. It is not the Vetus Latina. There are correspondences with all these, but they are haphazard.

I owe to Andrew Brown the identification of the main, black text as the new translation, 'intelligentia ex Graeco' in all its purity, of Jacques Lefèvre d'Etaples. Assuming that Meghen followed his usual practice of copying from a printed book, this means that the manuscript must have been transcribed after 1512, when Lefèvre's version was first published, at Paris. There was a second edition in 1515. Sample collations have not revealed which edition was used. Nor is it clear what 'copy' exactly was handed to the scribe. Something fairly elaborate in the way of instruction, one assumes, would have been necessary. For the Vulgate and Lefèvre alone, it might have been managed with – say – an underlined copy of the printed text, where the versions are printed much after the style of the 'Colet' manuscripts of the New Testament, with the Vulgate – which, incidentally, Lefèvre believed in this instance to have been the work of an earlier translator than St Jerome – in the more substantial of two columns. The new version occupies the narrower column. Perhaps, also, the mysterious but intermittent other source could simply have been patched in according to readings supplied.

It would be good to know much more about knowledge and use of Lefèvre in England during the 1490s and the early years of the sixteenth century, and about contacts, intellectual and personal, between Lefèvre and Colet.[14] Born about 1460, Lefèvre was a considerable Greek scholar who had early, in Paris, made a strong humanist attempt to clear away Scholastic lumber from Aristotle. For this, he was praised in Thomas More's *Letter to Dorp* as the restorer of true dialectic and true philosophy, while his translation of St Paul was recommended to the Monk. The example of Ermolao Barbaro had encouraged Lefèvre to continue along the course he had set himself. On his first journey to Italy, he seems actually to have met the Platonic philosopher Marsilio Ficino, who influenced him in his dealings with the Platonic and Neoplatonic writings, including those of the writers who were then held to be Platonic witnesses, ps-Dionysius the Areopagite and Hermes Trismegistus. Becoming deeply involved with them, he later edited both. In Italy also, he met the great syncretist Giovanni Pico della Mirandola. In respect of these two meetings, it seems, he had the advantage of John Colet. Returning to Paris, he issued more paraphrases of and commentaries on Aristotle, in which he demonstrated, among other things, how closely Aristotelian and Christian doctrine were akin to one another.

There are obvious similarities in approach to the sacred text between Lefèvre and Erasmus. Lefèvre had read the *Annotationes* of Valla, and absorbed their lesson. Erasmus refers to him with great respect in his own *Annotationes*. They may have met before 1511, by which time Lefèvre had published his pioneer *Psalterium quintuplex*, his *Five-part Psalter* in 1509, in which he set beside one another five Latin versions, the Gallican, the Roman, and the translation according to the Hebrew, all three as made by St Jerome, together with the Old Latin and the so-called Conciliatum, the Vulgate text emended in a few places - a publication at once more specialized and more elaborate than Erasmus's *Novum Instrumentum* of seven years later. The *Psalterium quintuplex* is commended to Dorp by More. It figures in the library list that I have mentioned more than once, along with unspecified works by Lefèvre's disciples Clichthove and Bouelles.[15] Later, after the appearance of the *Novum Instrumentum*, there was bad blood between Erasmus and Lefèvre.

14 See *Contemporaries of Erasmus*, ii, Toronto, 1986, pp.315–8; and *The prefatory Epistles of Jacques Lefèvre d'Étaples and related Texts*, ed. Eugene F. Rice Jr., New York and London 1972, esp.pp.295–302.
15 British Library, Additional MS 40676.

It would be interesting if a connexion between Colet and Lefèvre could be established, but it has to be admitted that the proof is lacking, and it is true that the two are divided as to the Christian humanist position. Lefèvre holds rather to the view of Erasmus, that everything good in pagan literature is to be referred to Christianity. All is the result of pre-Christian revelation, in the attitude that D. P. Walker christened *prisca theologia*.[16] I believe that Colet, in his early days, was attracted to this attitude, but that he abandoned it in later years. Entering the realms of pure conjecture, it might be said that the young Lefèvre was just making his Parisian reputation at the time when Colet first visited that city; that Robert Gaguin was known to Colet and to Lefèvre, as to More, having visited England in the 1490s – and even that Colet and Lefèvre were perhaps in Italy at the same time. There has always been a mystery about Colet's pilgrimage to that country. Could it have been Lefèvre that encouraged it?

We have no indication whatever that Colet and Lefèvre ever met, or even that Colet knew the work of Lefèvre, except for Lefèvre's edition of Ambrogio Traversari's Latin translation of the ps-Dionysius. They seem to have been at one in their continued belief in the apostolicity of the ps-Dionysius, the fifth-century Syrian mystic as he is now known to have been, long regarded as the convert of St Paul of Acts 17.34, and therefore for the Middle Ages and Renaissance a first-hand Christian-Platonic witness. Valla, as we have seen, and later Erasmus, with Nicolaus of Cusa, joined the chorus of know-alls – *scioli*, as Cardinal Bellarmine was later to call them – who cast doubt on the identification. For Marsilio Ficino, he was the crown and summit of Platonic doctrine and so he remained for Colet and Lefèvre. For each of them the *Celestial and Ecclesiastical Hierarchies* and not the *Divine Names* were the important texts. In the *Hierarchies* the mediation, the descent of divinity through the nine orders of angels in their due ranks, the fiery seraphim, the cherubim and the rest to the ordinary messengers, the angels

16 D. P. Walker, *The Ancient Theology: Studies in Christian Platonism from the Fifteenth to the Eighteenth Century*, London 1972, esp. pp.1–22.

tout court, and the continuance of this mediation through the hierarchy of the Church, were the important aspect of the message. The *Hierarchies* seem to have been well-known enough in sixteenth-century England. Lefèvre's edition of Traversari's translation (1498-9) was, indeed, a common book everywhere. The *Hierarchies* are, for example, twice mentioned in the library list I have spoken of already. Colet, it seems, never lost his sense of the profound importance of this descent of grace and illumination. One of his lost and last works was the sermon he preached at Wolsey's receipt of the red hat, cardinals corresponding to cherubim. The famous Convocation Sermon of 1511 is full also of the imagery and the spirit of the ps-Dionysius. Lefèvre, too, clung to the anti-Valla position. Colet's continued belief is perhaps the more remarkable in that not long before the time when he had the draft of his *Abbreviations* of the ps-Dionysius copied out fair by Pieter Meghen, William Grocyn had been lecturing on the ps-Dionysius in London. This seems to have been in about 1500. Grocyn had got well into his stride when he came on Valla and was convinced by him that the Pauline, apostolic figure was a fiction. He forthwith cancelled the rest of the series.

Grocyn may well have been using a Greek text of the ps-Dionysius, who was by this time widely available in more than one Latin translation. Lefèvre could have done the same. He also made more generally current what became the standard Renaissance translation of the *Celestial and Ecclesiastical Hierarchies*. This had been completed in 1436 by the Camaldolese monk, Ambrogio Traversari. Traversari's was the version that Colet used when he came to make his *Abbreviations* of ps-Dionysius. Moreover he used it, not in the first edition of Bruges 1480, but in the second, edited by Lefèvre and printed at Paris in 1498-9.[17] Like almost all Colet's works, these *Abbreviations* were not printed until the nineteenth century.[18] They are nevertheless the

---

17 Eugene F. Rice, Jr., *Renaissance News*, xvii, 1964, pp.108-9; and see J. B. Trapp, 'John Colet and the *Hierarchies* of the ps-Dionysius', *Studies in Church History*, xviii, 1982, pp.127-48. For the influence of the ps-Dionysius on Colet see still E. W. Hunt, *Dean Colet and his Theology*, London 1956.

18 Edited by J. H. Lupton, 1869-76.

Jo. Colet de Angelis celestiq̃ breuarchia ferũ Dyonisium

Cognosco tuam sublimem et angelicam mentem vir optime
& amice charissime; digña sane; que non solum de angelis
audiat. sed preterea que cum ipis vna consocietur. Quappter
que heri ac nudius tercius apud Dyonisium Arriopagitam
in eo suo libro qui inscribitur de celesti hierarchia; In quo
magnifice & diuinitus de angelis disseuit / legi & memoria
repotaui; ea uolo tecum communicare. quũ in reportatis
& in hijs que dedicimus in eo libro. id uel primũ et maxi:
mum est; vt quicquid aliunde accepimus boni; id benigniter
deinceps impartiamus alijs & communicemus. hoc imitati
inestimabilem dei bonitatem; qui largiter se & ordine com:
municat vniuersis, quiq̃ dat, quicquid dat ve demde cui
datur ab eodem euestigio traditur alij; quatenus posset continua
ab alio in alium distributis & diriuatis donis dei. vmiuer:
si & deum bonum agnoscat. et ipsi simul diuina bonitate
concopulentur. Itaq̃ habe nũc que memoria mea refer:
uauit ex illa dyonisiaca lectione; que breuiter capitorũ
ordinem secutus & summatim sic perstringere ꝓ tempore.
capite est;a pre illo luminũ exire & p conditas res erna:
nare candidam quamdam & spiritalem lucem rerum om:
rium quatinus sua cuiusq̃ natura patitur; in se reuocatri:
cem. ve sistat se quodq̃ ordine & gradu suo, ac pro modo
sue nature in deo perficiatur. Lux autem illa vna per oĩa
& penitus simplex est. non uariata rerum varietate; sed varia sunt & diuisa
ria quoad fieri potest in similitudinem; in qua vnitate sui.
vnitate lucis omnino & idemtitate est uarietas rerum
ut sint confusione semp uarietate eadem manet vna
& in simplex in varijs reb

Aaj

only works of Colet's which we possess in three recensions, one of them unknown to their heroic nineteenth-century editor, so that of them all the *Hierarchies* are most badly in need of a new edition. First there is the paper manuscript, part autograph, part corrected transcript, now MS Gg. iv. 26 in Cambridge University Library (Fig.42). From this was transcribed, by Pieter Meghen some time before 1517, the vellum manuscript formerly owned by the Duke of Leeds, and long before him by Lord Burghley, whose arms can be seen on its binding. It was sold in the auction that included so many books from Burghley's library in 1687.[19] Now, it is Additional MS 63853 in the British Library. It also contains the treatise *De sacramentis ecclesiae*.[20] In this manuscript there are substantial additions and corrections, some by Colet, using a brown-tinted ink, and some by another hand (Fig.43), very like Colet's but larger and bolder than Colet's rapid, smaller writing (Fig.44), and using red ink. This second hand has annotated the *Ecclesiastical Hierarchy*, as is common in the manuscripts and printed editions of the ps-Dionysian *Hierarchies* that I have seen: clerical concern was less with those beings of the upper world and their ranks and operations, than with their flesh-and-blood counterparts on earth, the clergy in their proper stations. The hand may be Tunstal's, a proposition made nearly a century ago which I am still, after twenty years' hesitation, not quite yet prepared to accept.[21] I have, on the other hand, not yet found a convincing alternative candidate. The third manuscript, of both the *Hierarchies*, is the mid-sixteenth-century codex now at St Paul's School. It is on paper and is imperfect, a couple of sheets having been torn out of the *Ecclesiastical Hierarchy*. It incorporates the additions and corrections made in Additional MS 63853, and it was used by Lupton for his edition.

19 *Bibliotheca illustris: sive Catalogus variorum librorum . . .*, London 1687, p.89, lot 119. Another manuscript written by Meghen which was once in Burghley's possession is now Rawlinson MS A.431 in the Bodleian Library.

20 Now ed. with a translation in John B. Gleason, *John Colet*, Berkeley etc. 1989, pp.270–333.

21 M. R. James, *A descriptive Catalogue of the Manuscripts in Corpus Christi College, Cambridge*, ii, Cambridge 1911, p.187.

If the hand that annotated Additional Ms 63583 in red is indeed not Colet's, I have some explaining to do. 'To lose one parent, Mr Worthing', as Lady Bracknell immortally remarked, 'may be regarded as a misfortune. To lose both seems like carelessness.' Similarly, I have to ask for indulgence in my explanation of why I believe that neither of two extant copies of the Statutes of St Paul's School, compiled by Colet, and each bearing the twice repeated assertion that it is inscribed by him *manu propria*, provides any trace of Colet's hand.

The hand is certainly that of someone closely connected with Colet. I think I have identified it on documents relating to Colet's lands and other property. Is it therefore the hand of an executor? Whether that be so or not, it is certainly the same hand as wrote the rather cross note in another Meghen manuscript of some of Colet's works, now Corpus Christi College, Cambridge MS 355: 'Supersunt multa ab eodem Joannis Colet scripta in diuum paulum sed puerorum eius incuria perierunt', 'There were many more surviving of these writings of John Colet's, but they have been lost through the carelessness of his boys (i.e. the boys of St Paul's School?) or servants' (Fig.45). If this is indeed the hand of an executor, it is not – incidentally – the hand of Colet's mother, Dame Christian, who on such documents as I have seen can manage only to scratch her initials and seal them.

The sixteenth-century state of the Statutes of St Paul's School is attested by more than a dozen copies, including nineteenth-century transcripts. All but one are at Mercers' Hall.[22] The earliest text represented at Mercers' Hall is a paper manuscript bound in vellum. Painted on its front cover is a replica of Colet's tomb in Old St Paul's, ascribed to Sir William Segar (Fig.48). The binding is usually dated about 1585. Supplementary statutes of 1602 and 1841 have been inserted.[23] Textually, this Mercers' Hall manuscript dates from 1517, though the actual manuscript

22 I owe thanks to Jean Imray and her successor as Mercers' Archivist, Anne Sutton.
23 F. Grossmann, 'Holbein, Torrigiano and Portraits of Dean Colet: A Study of Holbein's Work in Relation to Sculpture', *Journal of the Warburg and Courtauld Institutes*, xiii, 1950, pp.202–36; '*King's good Servant*', no. 12.

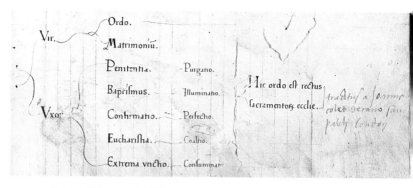

43 British Library, Additional MS 63583, fol. 140v.

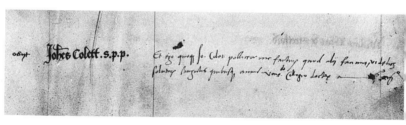

44 Lambeth Palace Library, MS D.C.1, fol. 11.

may not have been transcribed until later, after Colet's death. On its flyleaf it is annotated in red by – I believe – the hand that wrote the red annotations in Additional MS 63853 and Corpus Christi College, Cambridge MS 355: 'hunc libellum ego Joannes Colet tradidi manubus magistri lilij xviij° die Junij anno Christi M.CCCCCxviij vt eum in scola seruet et obseruet'; p. 1 has the subscription 'Joannes Colet fundator scole manu sua propria' (Fig. 46); and at the foot of the text on p. 22, the last text page, there is again 'Joannes Colettus fundator noue scole manu mea propria'. These superscriptions, despite their wording, are not in Colet's hand; they must have been copied on to the Mercers' Hall MS at some later stage.

45 Cambridge, Corpus Christi College, MS 355, fol. 194.

46 London, Mercers' Hall, Statutes of St Paul's School, fol. 1.

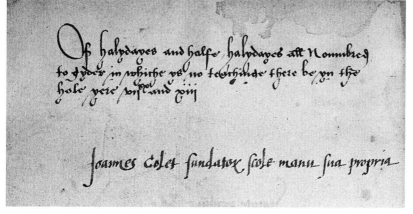

47 London, British Library, Additional MS 6274, fol. 1v.

IO COLET DECA[...] S PAVLI

ISTVC RECIDIT GLO
RIA CARNIS

48 London, Mercers' Hall, Statutes of St Paul's School, Binding.

The only manuscript of the Statutes not in the possession of the Mercers' Company is Additional MS 6274 in the British Library. It differs textually from the Mercers' Hall MS and seems to represent an earlier state, of perhaps 1512, just when the School had been completed. On the other hand, the evidence of its script points to its having been transcribed at some time towards the middle of the sixteenth century. The record of the School's endowment at the conclusion of the main text is less full than in the Mercers' Hall MS; conversely, there is a clause about 'remedies', holidays, which is not in the Mercers' Hall MS. The superscriptions of the Mercers' Hall MS have been copied faithfully in the identical positions, by a hand that is even less to be identified with Colet's than that of the Mercers' Hall MS (Fig.47).

The hand that annotated those three manuscripts in red is also, I believe, the hand which annotated a late-fifteenth-century book of hours in the Ghent-Bruges style, now at Stonyhurst and once the property of Katherine, wife of Sir Reynold Bray, one of Henry VII's substantial supporters. It may have passed to Colet on Dame Katherine's death in 1507. Above its miniature of the *Raising of Lazarus* there is the red-ink injunction to pray for Colet's soul, which can hardly have been written by Colet himself.[24]

The Statutes of St Paul's School are interesting for reasons other than these.[25] Colet had made his first moves towards founding the School soon after his father's death, obtaining the mortmain licence for the erection of a new building on church ground in 1508, and making conveyance of the lands of its endowment to the Mercers. In 1512 all was ready, and William Lily in post as first High Master. Colet was at work, one assumes, on his *Aeditio*, the accidence in English which he wrote for the School and and which he recommends for its use, unless another 'be better to the purpose to induce chyldren more

24 I am grateful to Jonathan Alexander for showing me photographs of this manuscript. See now his 'Katherine Bray's Flemish Book of Hours', *The Ricardian*, viii, no. 107, 1989, pp.308–17 and esp.fig. 1.
25 They are most conveniently available in J. H. Lupton, *Life of John Colet,* 2nd ed., London 1909, pp.271–84.

spedely to laten spech'. No edition from Colet's lifetime survives. Both the preface to the *Aeditio*[26] and the Statutes declare themselves in favour of the humanist-grammatical mode of learning Latin and Greek – and not those languages 'alonely': the 153 boys are to be instructed in good manners and good Christian life. Their grammar was to be got by much reading and exercise, not by cramming of its rules:

> For in the begynnynge men spake not latyn bycause suche rules were made, but contrariwyse bycause men spake suche latyn upon that folowed the rules were made. That is to saye, latyn speche was before the rules, not the rules before the latyn speche.

The boys were to pray regularly, and they were to have as their guide to moral behaviour not only the Catechism, but also the *Institutum christiani hominis* of Erasmus, the Creed, essentially, with a strong Augustinian injection of duty to God, to neighbour and to oneself. To assist them to more fluency, both in matter and in style, they had Erasmus's *De duplici copia verborum ac rerum* – *Reciprocal Abundance in Words and Matter*, which Erasmus had written specially for the School. Later, he was to complain that Colet had not stumped up enough for the dedication. There were also grammars, though these get no precise specification in the Statutes. Linacre's attempt having early been rejected as too advanced, Lily and Erasmus's joint production – which neither was willing to own after the work of one had been revised by the other – seems soon to have been adopted;[27] and others of Lily's works were in use: his little treatise on nouns and verbs and his *Carmen de moribus*.

The paragraph on 'What shalbe taught' in the Statutes (Fig.49), of which the above is a paraphrase, opens with a general disclaimer and prescription:

> As towchyng in this scole what shalbe taught of the Maisters and lernyd of the scolers it passith my wit to devyse and

26 Reprinted in Lupton, *Life of Colet*, pp.290–2.
27 *STC2*, no. 15610.

What shalbe taught

As towchyng in this scole what shalbe taught of the Maisters and lernyd of the scolers it passith my wyt to devyse and determyn in particuler but in genrall to speke and sum what to saye my mynde I wolde they were taught all way in good litterature both laten and greke and goode auctors suych as haue the veray Romayne eloquence joyned wyth wysdome specially Cristen auctours that wrote theyre wysdome with clene and chast laten other in verse or in prose for my entent is by thys scole specially to incresse knowlege and worshyppyng of god and oure lorde Crist Iesu and good Cristen lyff and maners in the Children And for that entent I will the Chyldern lerne ffyrst above all the Cathechyzon in Englysh and after the accidence that I made or sum other yf eny be better to the pporse to induce children more spedely to laten spech And thenne Institutum Christiani hominis which that lernyd Erasmus made at my request and the boke called Copia of the same Erasmus And thenne other auctors Cristian as Lactancius prudentius and proba and sedulius and Iuuencus and Baptista Mantuanus and suche other as shalbe taught convenyent and moste to pporse vnto the true laten spech all barbary all corrupcion all laten adulterate which ignorant blynde folis brought into this worlde and with the same hath distayned and poysonyd the olde laten spech and the veray Romayne tong which in the tyme of Tully and Salust and Virgill and Terence was vsid.

Marginal notes:
Cathechizacion
Acciakha
Institutum Xa hois
Copia verbor
Lactatius
Prudentius
Proba
Sedulius
Iuuencus
Bapta Mātua

49 London, Mercers' Hall, Statutes of St Paul's School, p. 13.

determyn in particuler but in generall to speke and sum what
to saye my mynde, I wolde they were taught all way in good
litterature both laten and greke, and goode auctors suych as
haue the veray Romayne eliquence joyned with wisdome
specially Cristyn auctours that wrote theyre wysdome with
clene and chaste laten other in verse or in prose, for my entent
is by thys scole specially to increase knowlege and
worshipping of god and our lord Crist Jesu and good Cristen
lyff and maners in the Children . . .

and, Colet goes on, let them read such authors

as shalbe thoughte convenyent and moste to purpose vnto the
true laten spech all barbary all corrupcion all laten adulterate
which ignorant blynde folis brought into this worlde and with
the same hath distayned and poysenyd the olde laten spech
and the varay Romayne tong which in the tyme of Tully and
Salust and Virgill and Terence was vsid, whiche also seint
Jerome and seint ambrose and seint Austen and many hooly
doctors lernyd in theyr tymes. I say that ffylthynesse and all
such abusyon which the later blynde worlde brought in which
more ratheyr may be callid blotterature thenne litterature I
vtterly abbanysh and exclude oute of this scole and charge the
Maisters that they teche allway that is the best and instruct the
chyldren in greke and laten in redying vnto them suych
auctours as hathe with wisdome joyned the pure chaste
eloquence.

If one is inclined to think that this is a humanist programme,
one is brought up short by the block of named authors which
ensues: Lactantius, Prudentius, Proba, Sedulius, Juvencus and
Baptista Mantuanus. Some of them, it is true, had been praised
by Erasmus, in one context or another.[28] Lactantius was the
Christian Cicero; Prudentius, according to Erasmus, in the *De
ratione studii* of 1511 – which comes as near as makes no matter
to a blueprint for the study modes of St Paul's School – was the
only stylish Christian poet, a kind of Christian Virgil. Proba,
the only woman author cited, was a learned fourth-century

28 Letter 49; Allen, i, p.163; *Correspondence*, i, pp.103–4.

compiler of a Virgilian Gospel narrative cento, of which Erasmus disapproved as a piece of patchwork keeping boys from the *ipsissima verba*.[29] Sedulius and Juvencus were fourth- and fifth-century versifiers of the New Testament. The only modern was a near-contemporary of Colet's and Erasmus's, the exemplary and much admired Mantuan, the Carmelite Bl. Baptista Spagnuoli of Mantua (1447–1516), another Christian Virgil.[30]

There may lie behind the recommendation of the poets that make up all but one of the authors thus specifically mentioned, their value as demonstrators of the techniques of metaphrase. They had put prose, in this case the prose of the Gospel narratives, into verse. This can be a secondary consideration only, however. What has happened is that, after the precise prescription of the works essential for good Christian life and manners, the Catechism and the *Institutum Christiani hominis*, and for sound knowledge of the style and the content of the classics, Colet has modulated into generality. The string of authors that begins with Lactantius was surely never intended to prescribe the authors who were actually to be read – as indeed there is no evidence that any of them except Mantuan were actually read. The early Christian poets were readily available, in recent editions from the Aldine press, for example.[31] The *Eclogues* of Mantuan were later to figure large in the St Paul's School syllabus, having become a popular schoolbook and been translated into more than one European language.[32] Their vogue in the North, in particular, however, is linked with their criticism of Curia and clergy, and they come fully into their kingdom in a Reformation context. To take it that Colet has them exclusively in mind here is to yield too readily to the nineteenth-century concept of Colet as a Reformer *avant-la-lettre*, one of the Fathers of the Anglican church. His reference is rather to the

---

29 Letter 32; Allen, i, p.125; *Correspondence*, i, p.62.
30 John F. D'Amico, *Contemporaries of Erasmus*, ii, Toronto 1986, p.375; Erasmus, Letter 47; Allen, i, p.157; *Correspondence*, i, p.97.
31 *Poetae christiani veteres*, 1501–2.
32 Edmondo Coccia, *Le edizioni delle opere del Mantovano*, Rome 1960; *Adulescentia. The Eclogues of Mantuan*, ed. with an English trans. by Lee Piepho, New York and London 1989.

whole prolific Christian *oeuvre* of Mantuan, in which the longer poems – the *Parthenicae*, poems on the Virgins, Mary and martyrs, for example – bulk larger than the *Eclogues*.

Colet's general prescription of named authors, before he passes to even greater generality, is both severe on the pagan classics and impractical. His letter to Erasmus soon after the foundation of St Paul's School perhaps even hints that the prescription was immediately disregarded, at least as to the authors to be read: the School, he wrote, had been called, and by a bishop at that, a useless, evil institution, 'a home of idolatry' and the abode of devils, because the poets were being taught there.[33] Later the standard classical authors certainly took over.[34] Colet himself intended his School to provide an education on up-to-date humanist lines, but an education which would also preserve its beneficiaries from the threat of pagan taint, in a much more restrictive sense – in terms of Christian humanism – than the understanding of Erasmus or of Lefèvre.

The intensity of Colet's fear of non–Christian sentiment may be somewhat exaggerated in the various accounts given by Erasmus of the intellectual encounters between the two. There was that incident concerning the *Antibarbari*, for which we have the word of Erasmus only.[35] Similarly, our record of the two famous disputes in Oxford during Erasmus's first visit to England in 1499 is substantially Erasmus's. One of the debates arose at table. It concerned Cain and Abel and the reasons why one brother's sacrifice should have been acceptable to God, while the other's was not. The consensus view was that Abel's blood sacrifice complied with divine precept. Cain merely brought to the altar what he wished to bring and not what God wished to have. Colet took an individual line, insisting – as ever – on absolutes: Cain's sin was that he had been a cultivator, an

33 Letter 258; Allen, i, p.508; *Correspondence*, ii, p.224.
34 T. W. Baldwin, *William Shakspere's small Latine and lesse Greeke*, Urbana, Ill. 1944.
35 Letter 1110; Allen, iv, p.279; *Correspondence*, vii, p.305; and cf. *Collected Works of Erasmus*, xxiii = *Literary and Educational Writings*, i, Toronto 1978, pp.8–9, 16.

improver, not a herdsman content with what God had given by way of provender for men and animals and so prepared to render thanks in those terms. Erasmus, thinking to lower the temperature of the discussion, essayed a facetious explanation of how Cain had come to be such a successful agriculturalist: it is doubtful whether Colet appreciated the attempt.[36] Likewise, the account of a more extended and serious debate, concerning the Agony in the Garden, is from Erasmus's pen.[37] Colet, he tells us, advanced a characteristically individual and recondite explanation of the reason for the sweat of blood of Christ in Gethsemane and his plea that the cup should pass from him. The consensus opinion among commentators from the Fathers onwards was the commonsense one: the human element in Christ's nature was asserting itself against the divine: his kinship with man was being expressed in the fear of death. For Colet, this view was a derogation from the divinity of Christ: his divine perfection could not have admitted that human weakness. The sweat and the cry could only have been the result of Christ's consciousness of the guilt that the Jews were about to bring upon themselves in compassing his death. It is not clear whether Colet had excogitated this view himself – nor indeed whether the same is true of his explication of the sacrifice of Cain and Abel – or whether he had found it in the one patristic commentator in whom it occurs. St Jerome, as Erasmus points out, had advanced it once only, but had later abandoned it in favour of the consensus view. The weighing of authorities, here as in philology, was what counted for Erasmus. In the words of Thomas More almost twenty years later, in 1516, Colet's way was 'for the sake of argument, to resist those who try to persuade him, even if their point is one to which he is strongly inclined of his own accord'.[38]

36 Letter 116; Allen, i, pp.268–71; *Correspondence*, i, pp.229–33.
37 Letters 108–111; ibid., pp.245–60; 202–19; and see Erasmus, *Disputatiuncula de tedio, pavore, tristicia Jesu* . . . in *Lucubratiunculae*, first published at Antwerp 1503; but see Colet's retort, not printed until the edition of Erasmus's *Lucubratiunculae*, Basel 1518; Erasmus, *Opera omnia*, ed. J. Leclerc, Leiden 1703–6, v, cols. 1291–4.
38 Letter 468; Allen, ii, p.347; *Correspondence*, iv, p.80.

To speak of authorities, what did Colet read? We have seen that there is little to be gleaned from his will, and that there is no extant library list. The most recent study, an excellent book by John B. Gleason, has a valuable list of 'certain or probable references', in addition to the Bible, to the ps-Dionysius, with whose *Hierarchies* we have already seen that Colet was thoroughly familiar, and Marsilio Ficino, of whom there is more to say. Erasmus's famous and very moving obituary letter mentions in particular the Scholastics, specifying Scotus and Aquinas, as well as Cicero, Plato, Plotinus, ps-Dionysius, Origen, Cyprian, Ambrose, Jerome and Augustine and – surprisingly – the English poets, whose works helped to give him that fluency in preaching for which he was to become famous.[39] Naturally, Erasmus makes no mention of himself, though Colet everywhere makes up for this by acknowledging his debt.[40]

There can be no doubt that Colet knew his Scholastics well. He had, after all, been through the university mill, at Cambridge. As to the Fathers mentioned by Erasmus, with the famous comment that Colet was 'iniquior' – a little harder on – Augustine, Augustine is, on Gleason's count, the most frequently cited, together with Origen. Concerning Origen, there is a problem, which I shall deal with later. Concerning Augustine, it needs to be said that there is a great deal more of him in Colet than appears on the surface, especially if one is speaking in terms of diffused influence. Of Jerome, the only actual evidence is that Colet owned Erasmus's edition of his works and knew one of his New Testament Commentaries – provided always that he had not arrived at his view of the Agony in the Garden by his own route. Precise knowledge of Cyprian and Ambrose is not identifiable, though it would be surprising if he did not know them.

The same is true of the pagan authors that Erasmus notes: Cicero, Plato and Plotinus. Plato and Plotinus are both cited in

39 It seems to me at least possible that, at this remove in time, Erasmus was mixing up his two great English friends: More's knowledge of the English poets is undoubted and his English writings teem with reminiscences of Chaucer in particular; Colet's, on the face of it, is more problematic.
40 Letter 1211; Allen, iv, pp.507–27; *Correspondence*, viii, pp.225–44.

Colet's longer Commentary on Romans. The reference to Plato is a glancing one and may very well not be direct. It concerns the wisdom of the deity in framing the great body of the world – 'the animal, as Plato calls it' (in the *Timaeus*, 30D) – so that all living creatures in succession within the machinery of the universe are hierarchically locked into each other in such a way that none can dispense with the other. 'Animal' is the rendering of Plato's 'zoon' in Calcidius as well as in Marsilio Ficino's Latin translation of Plato, first printed in 1484; or Colet might have encountered it in Cicero. It was by that time such common doctrine that a reference to an ultimate source tells us little. Moreover, it occurs in a very Ficinian passage of the Commentary, at chapter xii. Similarly, the reference to Plotinus is a glancing reference only, in the Commentary at chapter vi, to the dominance of the animal part in post-lapsarian man – and Lupton more than a century ago showed it to have been through Ficino's Latin version of Plotinus, first published at Florence in 1492. It is clear that, even as late as 1516, whatever Colet knew of these Greek philosophers, as of Greek authors in general, he conformed very much to sixteenth-century type in knowing them only indirectly or through Latin translation.[41]

Other authorities are referred to in the context of the figurative interpretation of Scripture, among them the *Letter of Aristeas*, which had been available in print in the Latin translation by Matteo Palmieri since 1467 at latest.[42] Colet's allusion is to the *Letter's* account of the copiousness of Jewish blood sacrifice,

41 On Colet's late attempts to learn the language, see Thomas More to Erasmus, Letter 468; Allen, ii, p.347: 'At Coletus iam graecatur strenue, vsus in ea re precaria opera Clementis mei; credo fore vt pergat et peruadat nauiter . . .'; and *Correspondence*, iv, p.80: 'Colet is very busy with his Greek, in which he has the voluntary help of my friend Clement. I think he will make progress and achieve his aim through hard work . . .'; and cf. Erasmus to Reuchlin, Letter 471; Allen, ii, p.351: 'Scribe vel paucis Coleto; is iam senex graecatur'; and *Correspondence*, iv, p.87: 'Send Colet a letter, even a short one; old man as he now is, he is learning Greek.'
42 *Editio princeps* in the edition of St Jerome's *Epistolae* printed at Rome, not later than 1467: *GW*, 2330; see British Library, *Incunable Short Title Catalogue*, London 1990.

which he interprets as the blind sign and token of the living sacrifice of the body to which we are exhorted by St Paul.[43] To Philo Judaeus, on the other hand, his reference is also almost certainly indirect: he merely asserts, in parentheses, that Philo says that Moses had believed the world to be eternal.[44]

Like his views on most subjects, Colet's views on Scripture interpretation were highly individual. He was far from scouting the multiple senses, or the assistance that might be got from the Old Testament, though he always insisted that those senses could and should not be identified before one had a thorough grasp of the literal meaning. All would later come together in that final, unitary message that ensures true piety. He gives a diverting illustration from the hierarchy of the brute creation, likening it to a hierarchy of interpretation. Just as, he says, the lowest orders swarm, and flies – for example – breed by hundreds and thousands so, as you mount the ladder, the number of offspring declines. When you arrive at the most exalted of all winged creatures, the eagle, you arrive at a brood of one. So literature may be interpreted in as many senses as you like, but the true, the vital and life-giving sense of Scripture will be single and refulgent.[45]

It has already been suggested that a strong presence of the pagan classics is not to be expected in Colet. A passing reference or two to Ovid, Terence and Virgil in addition to what has already been mentioned will almost exhaust the total. One striking and perhaps unexpected reference is, however, to the Roman historian whom we have already seen to be a chief source for Roman Imperial exemplary history. In his longer Commentary on Romans, Colet uses Suetonius to set the Epistle

---

43 *Lectures on Romans*, chap.12, ed. Lupton, London 1873, p.177.

44 *Letters to Radulphus*, 1, ed. Lupton, London 1876, p.168. Though the *De mundo* was available in print, in Greek, in the *editio princeps* of Aristotle, no Latin translation of any work by Philo was printed before Colet's death.

45 See Colet's reply to Erasmus on the Agony in the Garden, in Erasmus, *Lucubratiunculae*, 1518; ed. Leclerc, Leiden 1703–6, v, col. 1291; and cf. *Ecclesiastical Hierarchy*, v.1: Introduction to Orders, in Colet, *Super opera Dionysii*, ed. Lupton, London 1869, pp.232–42.

in context.[46] Whether he got the Epistle's date of composition right or wrong is beside the point. The important thing is that he is seeing the particular passage as a response to a given historical situation in so far as it is advice to Christians as to how to behave under a fickle ruler and in a pagan context, counselling them against contention either with authority or among themselves, and exhorting them to good behaviour both as something desirable in itself and as a protection against persecution. There is a sense in which he is here following the humanist-oriented advice he had passed on from Rome in 1493 to Christopher Urswick, in the letter he prefixed to the manuscript of Aeneas Sylvius Piccolomini and Leonardo Bruni Aretino.

Erasmus makes no mention of Suetonius among the authors Colet knew and used. Apart from the Scholastics, he gives no clue, either, to Colet's reading in post-classical authors. Among these the two dominant names are Giovanni Pico della Mirandola and Marsilio Ficino. The former we know from internal evidence alone that he read; of the latter we have one of the rare survivals from Colet's own library, the only printed book we know that he owned to have come down to us. His copy of Ficino's *Epistolae* bears ample evidence of passionate reading and marking.

Pico is not infrequently met with in England at the time under discussion, both at royal level and in less elevated circles. As we shall see, however, Colet seems to have been the only early Tudor Englishman to have been fired by his eclectic philosophy rather than by his *piagnone* piety. In his pious manifestation Pico is to be found among the Royal manuscripts, in French, dedicated to Henry VII; and he was translated into English both by Thomas More and by Sir Thomas Elyot.

A quarter of a century ago, Roberto Weiss took a first sounding.[47] William Melton, the tutor of John Fisher, owned a

---

46 *Lectures on Romans*, ed. Lupton, London 1873, pp.95–7, 201.

47 'Pico e l'Inghilterra', *L'opera e il pensiero di Giovanni Pico della Mirandola nella storia dell'umanesimo: Convegno internazionale, Mirandola 15–18 settembre 1963*, Florence 1965, i, pp.143–58; and see the further information in George B. Parks, 'Pico della Mirandola in Tudor Translation', *Philosophy and*

copy of the *Heptaplus*; there was a Pico at Corpus Christi College, Oxford in 1517, and John Claymond, its first President, later gave the College a copy of Pico's *Opera* of 1496. In 1520–1, the Oxford bookseller John Dorne sold a Pico for 3s4d; Bryan Rowe, Vice-Provost of King's College, Cambridge, had acquired a copy of the *Opera* before his death in 1521; volumes of his works were in the library at Syon before 1526. These are bare and not very enlightening facts. When we come to ask what English understanding and use of Pico was we are at once in difficulties, as so often when we seek to get books off library shelves or out of library lists, to get them open and follow their contemporary readers through their encounters with the words written or printed in them, with their ideas and what was made of them. About the same time as Weiss made his cautious chronicle, Frances Yates proposed that Pico's studies in the 'secret misteryes of the hebrewes, caldyes and arabies' and 'ye olde obscure philosophye of Pythagoras, trismegistus, and orpheus' had in some sense influenced Thomas More when he was describing the religion of the Utopians and their reverence to a 'Godlie powre unknowen, everlastinge, incomprehensible, inexplicable, far above the capacities and retche of mans witte . . . the father of al'. The Utopians, she believed, were *prisci theologi* all, prototypes of later religious Hermetism.[48] Despite the fact that Pico's name never occurs in More's *Utopia* and that Pico is never mentioned by his contemporaries in writing of More, Frances Yates's vision carries, as it always did, strong persuasions. We know, as I have already suggested, so little about More's ownership of books, particularly in his earlier days, and so much about his habit – in jest and in earnest – to conceal, that it is indeed possible that there is some broad and generalized influence from Pico in this instance. To return, however, to the demonstrable, the works of Pico's to which we know that More was attracted were not his *Conclusiones*, his

Humanism: Essays in Honor of Paul Oskar Kristeller, ed. Edward P. Mahoney, Leiden 1976, pp.352–69.
48 Frances A. Yates, *Giordano Bruno and the Hermetic Tradition*, London 1964, pp.185–7.

Apologia, his *Heptaplus*, his *De ente et uno*, his *Adversus astrologos*, which make up the bulk of the thick folio of his *Opera omnia*, nor even the brief *Oration on the Dignity of Man*. They were rather the *Life* of his philosopher uncle, written by Giovanni Francesco Pico and prefixed to the *Opera*, first published in 1496, and a little group of much briefer works still, letters of counsel and – still more popular about this time – three duodecalogues. These three sets of twelve commandments are accompanied by an exposition of Psalm XV, 'Preserve me, o Lord, for in Thee have I put my trust.' Three manuscripts of French translations of these, dedicated to Henry VII, are now among the Royal manuscripts in the British Library. One at least of these translations was completed by a French pupil-assistant of Erasmus's, one Germanus Amoenus Drocensis, on the basis of work begun by Henry Hault, priest and *utraque lingua peritus*, according to Bernardus Andreas, whose pupil he was. This manuscript, now Royal MS 16 E. XIV, was a New Year's gift for 1509; the other two Royal MSS, 16 E. XXIV and 16 E. XXV, may also, in their sententious brevity, have been intended for similar purposes. The duodecalogues begin with the twelve rules for spiritual battle against sin, pass to the twelve weapons for self-defence in the battle, including a consciousness of the fleetingness of pleasure and of the comfort of the Cross, and conclude with the twelve 'conditions of a lover', one-liners on loving God alone.

The three Royal manuscripts are in French, the contemporary language of culture. They are in part typical New Year's gifts, and in part typical of a pious taste which went much deeper and further than court circles (Fig. 50). Later, in the 1530s, Sir Thomas Elyot was to translate into English prose the rules for spiritual conflict. On this occasion, he was seeking less to demonstrate how the English language might be strengthened and augmented than merely to provide wholesome counsel for a female relative who had taken the veil after the death of her husband. His translation was printed with his translation of St Cyprian on man's mortality in 1534 and 1539; it was issued again with the works of Thomas Lupset in 1546 and 1560, and again in 1585 and 1615 with Richard Whitford's translation of the *Imitation of Christ*, which had been first published in 1531.

Doueuſe vierge
marie mere de dieu
treſmiſericordieuſe
humblement Je vo⁹
ſupplie que veuillez
deprier po⁹ moy
treſuil pecheur
deuat ſe regard de vre chier filz affin que to⁹
mes peches me ſoiet pardonnez ⁊ affin que tēps
de penitence me ſoit donē ⁊ ferme ppos damende
ment a promeriter laide de la grace diuine.
et tout tant quil me fault en regraciāt ſes
benefices de dieu: ſupplies po⁹ moy benigne
mere de miſericorde en offrant vous meiſmes
auecqs vre treſaymat et treſayme filz au
regard de la gloire paternelle: et que vre in-
tegrite virginale puiſſe excuſer mon ipurite
tāt de lame que du corps. Vre charite puiſſe
ēbraſer ma tepidite et negligence. Vre humi-
ſite puiſſe faire enclmer mon orgueil. et
vre obedience voluntaire puiſſe rompre et

50 London, British Library, Royal MS 16 E.XXIV, fol. 2.

The most considerable translation into English of any work connected with Pico, however, was Thomas More's version of Giovanni Francesco Pico's *Life*, along with three letters of Pico's concerning right conduct, his interpretation of Psalm XV, with prosy verse expansions of Pico on the rules and conditions of a lover and the weapons for spiritual battle and a longish prayer. All these translations were offered, also by way of New Year's gift, to a nun, Joyce Lee or Leigh. Elyot's translation was later also to be presented to a religious. When More's little book was put together, when the translations contained in it were made, is an open question. Perhaps, as has been suggested, not all at the same time.

More's version of the *Life* of Pico,[49] though it makes a rather more bulky New Year's gift than the other Pico translations so offered, is considerably abridged. More's selection is such as to make Pico's intellectual daring and ambition come a poor second to the piety that was leading him towards the monastery when he died. It may well be that Pico's syncretist spirit of tolerance, which also helped fuel his intellectual ambition, impressed More sufficiently for the memory of it to remain strong in his mind when he came to write the second book of *Utopia*. What is much more clear, in the letters of Pico's which More translated, is the germ of the 'dialogue of counsel' in the first book. In these, Pico is rejecting the idea of putting his learning at the disposal of a secular prince, and strengthening his nephew's resolution against the taunts of his former court associates. Clear also, in the letters as in the duodecalogues, is Pico's continuing preoccupation, which was also More's, with the need to resist the 'cuppes of Circe, that is to saie . . . the sensual affections of the flesh' by, among other things, the mortification of that flesh practised by both.

Sympathy with a morality that was both learned and austere, however, need not imply the correctness of the family tradition recorded in embellished form by Thomas More's great-grandson Cresacre More in 1626. Thomas Stapleton, in 1588, is

49 It will be the last volume to be published, though the first in numerical sequence, of the Yale Edition.

surely accurate in saying merely that More sought a model for the Christian layman's life in Pico; Cresacre More adds a corroborative detail that has bedevilled study ever since:

> When More determined to marry [i.e. about 1504] he propounded to himself, as a patterne of life, a singular layman John Picus Earl of Mirandula . . . [whose] life he translated and set out.

The glancing allusion – if indeed Cresacre More was aware of it – to Pico's reluctance to give up his mistress is perhaps less than fortunate. The implication as to timing, based on Cresacre More, taken years ago by A. W. Reed is equally suspect, on other grounds.[50] The translation was not, it seems, printed until 1510 or so, by More's brother-in-law John Rastell and, possibly about 1525, by Wynkyn de Worde. This tells us, unfortunately, nothing. We have no secure date for the writing, save for the first appearance of Gianfrancesco Pico's *Life* in 1496, and the probability that More was using its third edition of 1504. If More's translation of the *Life* was printed in 1510 it is the only one of More's works, with the exception of the Lucian of 1506 and 1514, which owed its publication rather to the force of Erasmus's name, to have been issued before *Utopia* in 1516; and the only one of his English works, with the possible exception of the *Merry Jest*, to have been printed before 1529.

As to Pico's *Opera*, it is likely that at least one copy was in English hands, and specifically in John Colet's, in the late 1490s. It is, I suppose, possible that this was the very copy also seen and used by More, though it looks as if the translation was made on the basis of the third edition, of Strasbourg 1504. Whatever edition was used, in other words, the Pico translation was the work of young manhood, when More's decision about his suitability for the religious life was being taken, and may or may not have to do with his marriage.[51] It was still a time when his Latin was less secure than it might have been. In one of the

50 *The English Works of Sir Thomas More*, i, London 1931, p.18.
51 I owe the information about the edition used to Nicolas Barker.

letters *mannus*, a Gallic coach-horse or cob, is translated as if it were *manus*, hand; and Paris is put for Perugia: hard words and not in the dictionary. Nor does the attempt to identify the nun help us greatly. It is known that Joyce Leigh was professed by 1507, by which time – in default of special conditions – she would have had to be sixteen years old. Her birth-date cannot therefore have been later than 1491; other evidence suggests that it may have been as early as 1474. I incline to the belief that she may have been a year or two younger than More, and therefore that she was born about 1480, though the possibility is that 1490 is the correct date, and the translations were made after More's marriage.

Gianfrancesco's *Life* of Pico had laid great stress on Pico's espousal of the contemplative life of resolute and purposeful scholarship, his renunciation of both family and official obligations, and his final intent to take the monastic habit, the Dominican dress in which he was buried. More left out about a seventh of what the nephew had to say, much of it concerning Pico's scholarship. This would presumably have been held irrelevant to the condition of an English nun, as would have been the discussion of marriage in one of the letters, which was also left out. The brief meditation on honour as virtue's continual companion rather than its mere antecedent, which More inserted, could clearly have had a general or a particular application.

For whatever purpose they were made, More's omissions affect the balance of Gianfrancesco's portrait of the life of learning gradually abandoned for religion's sake. The title-page of the English version as printed about 1525 (Fig. 51), with its Passion emblems, takes the process even further. In his translation, however, More did not entirely neglect the learned aspect of his subject: Pico's own reference in the letters to his enjoyment of 'my little house, my study, the pleasure of my bokes, the rest and peace of my minde' is allowed to stand; and so is what Pico says about the 'much watch and infatigable trauaile' with which he has 'learned both the Hebrew language, and the Chaldey: and nowe . . . set hand to ouercome the great difficultie of the Araby tonge.'

Here is coteyned the lyfe of Johan Picus
Erle of Myrandula a grete lorde of Italy an excellent
connynge man in all sciences/ & verteous of lyuynge.
With dyuers eppstles & other werkes of ý sayd
Johan Picus full of grete science vertue &
wysedome/whose lyfe & werkes bene
worthy & dygne to be redde
and often to be had in
memorye.

51 Giovanni Francesco Pico della Mirandola, *The lyfe of Johan Picus . . .*, translated Thomas More, London ?1525, Title-page.

Deciding just how far Pico's life of *pietas litterata* remained the ideal for More past the 1520s is difficult, and I have to confess that I have no real answer. His direct acquaintance with Pico's own works seems to be limited to the letters and maxims, though the case for his sharing some at least of Pico's intellectual attitudes seems a fair one. It is nevertheless difficult to see the *Life of Pico* as a humanist production: it is rather a not unconventional, not unsuitable New Year's gift for a religious, on the evidence of choice of passages for translation and the treatment of the text. On this showing, More is certainly no Hermetist.

The case of Colet is entirely different. There is no evidence that he owned Pico's *Opera* of 1496 or 1498, but it seems utterly plausible that he did so. The works that we know him to have read and used were available to him in print before the *Opera* were published, and he could have brought them back with him from his Italian journey – as he might have brought his copy of Marsilio Ficino's *Epistolae*, in the Venice edition of 1495. Much depends on when one believes Colet to have done most of his reading and writing, and my own view is that he probably did much less of both after he had come to London as Dean of St Paul's in 1505, or a little earlier. The case for his having used Lefèvre's edition of the *Hierarchies* of the ps-Dionysius, published in 1499, has been convincingly made, though of course he need not have used that edition exclusively (above, p. 106). On the other hand, his manuscripts seem to point to his having used no other. Our problem is compounded by the fact that we do not know precisely when the first, or the last, of the manuscript fair copies that Colet had made by Pieter Meghen of all his works were executed. The fair copies themselves, as we have seen, are amply corrected and rewritten. As far as extant evidence goes, all that can be said is that they were written after 1503 at the earliest, and not after 1517, on the evidence of the script. I believe that they were written one after the other, as a group, but there is no evidence even for that. Another scribe than Meghen was briefly at work on the manuscript which is now Corpus Christi College, Cambridge MS 355. At a guess, the most likely time would be between 1505 and say 1510, during which Meghen was also working for Colet on the grander New Testament manuscripts.

John Gleason has recently put all Colet's writings, in the form in which we now have them, at least, much later.[52] The *Abbreviations* of the *Hierarchies*, for example, he dates at 1512–16. They are certainly in the hand that Meghen used up to about 1517.[53] This would leave more than ample time for Colet to have used, for his knowledge of Pico, the *Opera* of 1496 or 1498 rather than earlier editions. Two observations may, however, be made. One is that, in 1517, Colet is expressing scepticism about Reuchlin's 'Pythagorical and Cabbalistic philosophy', in a letter to Erasmus, and recommending in its place, as the right way to the Dionysian purity, enlightenment and perfection, 'the fervent love and imitation of Christ'.[54] The *Abbreviation* of the *Ecclesiastical Hierarchy*, on the other hand, contains enthusiastic references to cabbala, and those references form part of a long direct quotation from Pico's *Apologia*. That particular passage, it ought also to be noted, also occurs verbatim in the famous *Oration on the Dignity of Man*. The *Apologia*, Pico's defence of his celebrated *Conclusiones* of 1486, the nine hundred theses on which he had invited public disputation for January 1487, was probably first printed in 1487. The *Oration* was not printed until Pico's nephew put it into the *Opera omnia*. If one accepts the view that Colet was using the *Opera omnia*, he might have taken his quotation from either the separate edition of the *Apologia* or the *Opera*. I have argued elsewhere that all Colet's references to cabbala are taken from Pico.[55] It seems more likely that cabbala, and Pico, occupy a phase of Colet's intellectual enthusiasm that had cooled considerably by 1516–7, when he was much more occupied, as Dean and member of the King's Council, with affairs of Church and state.

---

52 John B. Gleason, *John Colet*, Berkeley etc. 1989, pp.71–84.

53 Brown, loc. cit. n. 2 above.

54 Letter 593; Allen, ii, p.599; *Correspondence*, iv, p.398.

55 'A late medieval English Cleric and Italian Thought: The Case of John Colet, Dean of St Paul's, 1467–1519', *Medieval Religious and Ethical Literature: Essays presented to G. H. Russell*, Woodbridge 1986, pp.233–50; repr. *Essays on the Renaissance and the classical Tradition*, Aldershot 1990, no. xii.

I have also argued elsewhere that all Colet's references to the Greek Father whom Erasmus names among Colet's favourites are at second hand.[56] Whenever Colet cites Origen, the great Scriptural allegorist who happens to have been a favourite of Erasmus's, he is – I believe – either citing him through Pico, and perhaps Ficino, or he is picking up a relatively trivial reference from elsewhere. There is, nevertheless, no doubt of Origen's appeal for Colet, for his insistence on the principle of divine unity as for other things. The vogue for Origen comes in the 1510s, after the publication of the Latin *editio princeps* of 1512, though Latin manuscripts of some of his works had been long available. Rufinus's adaptation of the *De principiis* was not an uncommon book, and Cristoforo Persona's Latin translation of the *Contra Celsum* had been published in 1481. St Jerome's translation of Origen's *Homilies* into Latin was printed by Aldus in Venice in 1503. Some Origen was therefore available to Colet in Latin. Gleason's argument that Colet was brought to realize by the publication of the *Novum Instrumentum* in 1516 that he needed Greek in order to continue his exegetical work, and that he therefore began to learn it and had his earlier works written out fair as a sort of farewell to them, seems to me to be over-schematic. I believe that we must keep all Greek authors, in their original language, off Colet's library list. Though I can see a case – given Colet's will proved in the Court of Hustings in 1514 and his wish then to retire from the world, with St Paul's School fully founded and provided for – for seeing that particular moment as marking a stage when he felt his work was largely done, and though I can credit his being enthused by the appearance of the *Novum Instrumentum* a couple of years later, I find it difficult to see his 'collected edition' of his works as a memorial to his past life. The 'edition' seems to me rather a fair-copy-summation, prepared for continuance of work.

If Greek is out on the one hand, Pico, on the other, remains firmly in. The *Apologia*, or the *Oratio*, with the long passage on cabbala already mentioned, must certainly be there. So must the *Heptaplus*, Pico's seven-fold explanation of the seven days of

56 Op. cit., n. 55 above.

creation. The *Heptaplus* forms the basis of Colet's *Letters to Radulphus on the Mosaic Account of the Creation*.[57] There is also substantial use of it in the longer of Colet's two Commentaries on Romans,[58] as well as in his Sermon to Convocation of 1511.[59] Colet's view of the matter is decidedly less complicated than Pico's. Pico takes Moses to be telling of the creation of the three worlds of the macrocosm: the angelic-intellectual which exists above the spheres of the empyrean, inferior only to God himself; the celestial world of the planets; and the dull, elemental, sub-lunary, terrestrial world which mortals inhabit. Each of these worlds has its correspondences with the others, so that the gross, elemental fire of the sub-lunary world also exists in the celestial world, but in a purified form as the heat and light of the sun. It exists also in the empyrean, the supra-celestial world, where it is in its purest form of all, as the refined, perfected fire of the highest order of angels, the seraphic intelligences. To this three-fold macrocosm is also attached, by a series of correspond-ences, the microcosm, the little world of man, a fourth world. Pico treats the creation of these worlds in turn, one by one, day by day. Then he looks at them according to their differences from one another, and after that according to their similarities. Finally, arriving at the Lord's Day, he looks at them sabbati-cally, as they may be referred to Christ.

It is as easy as it is mistaken, in dealing with Colet as with More, to lose sight of a basically Aristotelian-Ciceronian-Augustinian formation and orientation – the sort of thing that no-one brought up at that particular time could have escaped – as one pursues the headier topics of Florentine neo-Platonic or syncretic philosophy. The *Letters to Radulphus*, for example, invite us to

> Mark how admirably he [that is to say Moses, the author
> of the Pentateuch] proceeds in order, in expressing the
> summary of creation, and the uniting of form with matter,

57 Ed. Lupton, London 1876.
58 Ed. Lupton, London 1873, pp.27, 73, 154, 185.
59 Lupton, *Life*, pp.293–304.

by his

opening words: *In the beginning*, that is, in eternity, *God created the heaven* [i.e. form] *and the earth* [i.e. matter].[60]

Colet, though expressly stating that he is following Pico 'the Platonist' in dividing the universe into four, adds an Aristotelian gloss which allows him to break Pico's sevenfold scheme. He ignores Pico's last four divisions and adds another, the divine, at the beginning. Colet's four divisions are: the eternal, immoveable, divine world; the equally eternal, but moveable world of the angels; the still eternal but sensible, celestial world of the planets; and the corruptible, sensible world of earth. Typically, Colet has eliminated the world of man, the mortal, corruptible world, and added the divine world. It is possible to see some influence from Ficino here. Pico usually stops at the angelic level, as in the *Heptaplus* and also in the *Commento alla canzone d'amore*.[61] Ficino more Neo-Platonically includes the divine level in any of his ontological schemes, four-, five- or six-fold, as in his Plato commentaries, especially those on the *Symposium* and the *Parmenides*, but also at the beginning of the third book of the *Theologia Platonica*, which Colet knew.[62] Ficino's four-fold scheme in his *Symposium* commentary is, however, not quite the same as Colet's.[63]

The doctrine of *spiritus* as the link between the immaterial soul and the material body of man, which is to be found both in the *Letters to Radulphus* and in Colet's Pauline commentaries, no-

60 Jill Kraye points out that Colet's formulation may have come direct from Pico, who had strong Aristotelian tendencies in common with Colet. See *Heptaplus, expositio prima*, chapter 2 = *Opera omnia*, Basel 1572–3, i, p.12, where what Pico is saying corresponds closely to Colet's sense.

61 *De hominis dignitate, Heptaplus . . . e scritti vari*, ed. E. Garin, Florence 1942, p.569.

62 Marsilio Ficino, *Théologie platonicienne . . .*, trans. and ed. R. Marcel, Paris 1964–70, i, pp.127–43.

63 Oratio vi, chaps. 15–17; *Commentaire sur le Banquet de Platon*, ed. R. Marcel, Paris 1956, pp.230–35. I owe these observations about Pico and Ficino and the references to Jill Kraye.

tably the longer Commentary on Romans, might likewise have come from Pico, either in the *Heptaplus* or the *Adversus astrologos*. Or it might have come from Marsilio Ficino.

Book-lists and surviving copies give some evidence for ownership of Ficino in early Tudor Britain. There is a copy of the 1491 edition of his Plato in the University Library at Durham; and there was a copy of Ficino's *Epistolae* in the library at Syon before 1526; Brian Rowe, the Vice-Provost of King's College, Cambridge, who died in 1521, owned a 'Ficinus parvum'. Ficino figures three times in British Library Additional MS 40676, and once among the books of the Benedictines of Monk Bretton, 1558. Colet is our first evidence of how he was read.

John Gleason has made the excellent suggestion that if we merely search for bits of Ficino that Colet used, we shall not find much that J. H. Lupton in the last century did not find (with the very great exception of the passages marked in Colet's copy of Ficino's *Epistolae*, of which more in a moment.) We shall also miss an important and, for that matter, an Erasmian-humanist similarity between their methods.[64] The full significance of the one extant book of Ficino's that we know once to have been in Colet's possession will also be obscured. This is the copiously annotated copy of Ficino's *Epistolae*, in the printing of Venice 1495, now in the Codrington Library at All Souls College, Oxford.[65] The *Epistolae* are brief expositions of philosophical topics rather than what would nowadays be known as letters. They are somewhat like the *argumenta* prefixed by Ficino to his translations of the books of Plato, first published about 1484; and used also in his version of Plotinus. An *argumentum*, Ficino says, 'seeks to bring out the whole argument in general terms and to get at its essence'; it is an interpretation, not a commentary. A commentator's duty is to make plain the meaning in detail; an interpreter seeks to bring out the significance. Colet makes the point himself to the young Edmund, to whom he is expounding Romans:

64 John B. Gleason, *John Colet*, Berkeley etc. 1989, pp.167–71.
65 Sears Jayne, *John Colet and Marsilio Ficino*, London 1963.

> The interpreter of Scripture need not act as a commentator
> does, and scrutinize words too minutely.[66]

Do that, and you are acting like the Scholastic commentators so despised by humanists, defining and distinguishing in their arrogant way, setting themselves up as superior to their texts. Your duty is to identify and expound the leading ideas, whether they are plain to see or hidden. If Colet is sometimes led into expatiating upon single words, and can be shown to have had a copy of Perotti's dictionary, the *Cornucopia*, in his hand as he did so, this is rare enough. Colet's merely lexical annotations are more sporadic than, say, Urswick's. He seems, indeed, unusual for his time in not having spent much ink on such activity. When he does so, he tends to expatiate, sometimes in a rather weird way, as in his explanations of *prevaricator* and *mentula*.[67]

To return to Ficino, the works that we can be entirely confident that Colet read are the *Theologia Platonica* and the *Epistolae*. Like St Paul, he was 'debtor both to the Greeks and the barbarians.'[68] He had been led by St Paul to Ficino and to Pico, in whatever order, as authorities, like the ps-Dionysius and like St Paul himself, on Platonism. Clearly, he was at that time in his career still prepared to accept as valid any truth from pagan philosophy that corresponded with Christianity. The pagans had their philosophers, he allowed, who took their knowledge from created things, the Jews had their prophets, angelically inspired: both may have got it right. Only, however, if it corresponded with Christian revelation could what they said be valid.

It is therefore no surprise to find Colet studying Ficino's *Theologia Platonica*, published in 1482, before his Platonic translations. By the time that Colet was philosophically aware enough to want to read him, Ficino was the acknowledged authority on the relations between Platonism and Christianity,

66 Quoted by Gleason, p.167.
67 Gleason, p.338.
68 Romans 1.14.

and on St Paul as Christian Platonist. A substantial, acknowledged chunk of the *Theologia Platonica* is inserted into the longer of Colet's interpretations of Romans, at 8.35, where St Paul is writing of the knowledge and love of God, and the superiority of love to knowledge, always a sympathetic concept for Colet, and specifically endorsed by Ficino:

> This much (says Colet), I have written, following Marsilio, concerning love's excellence . . . Marsilio, than whose philosophical expression there can be nothing finer.[69]

Colet's copy of the *Theologia Platonica* has disappeared. All the more reason to be grateful that Lupton's identification of Colet's borrowing from Ficino's *Epistolae* was confirmed, now almost forty years ago. This happened when Neil Ker discovered Colet's profusely annotated copy of the *Epistolae* in All Souls (Fig. 52). Over sixty of the *Epistolae* bear a total of some five thousand words of annotation, a quarry for assessing Colet's work both on St Paul and on the ps-Dionysius, as well as for his thought in general (Fig. 53). He annotates copiously, feverishly; he notes applications of Ficino to I Corinthians in particular;[70] he transcribes on a flyleaf a substantial letter written to him by Ficino but not printed in this or any other contemporary volume, in which Ficino is apparently replying to a question put to him by Colet concerning the differences between man's intelligence and his will.

When Colet summarizes Ficino, however, he transforms him in ways that are not always easy to define and characterize. The moral application, the application to life, always seems to bulk larger. He places strong emphasis on the ps-Dionysian stages of the soul's ascent through purification and illumination to perfection and union; on images of wholeness and oneness; on light. The speculative, intellectual dimension in Ficino is consistently reduced, as for example in what he says of those beings midway between divine and human, those whom Christians call angels

---

69 *Lectures on Romans*, pp. 29–32, 155–7.
70 See now *John Colet's Commentary on First Corinthians*, ed. B. O'Kelly and C. A. L. Jarrott, Binghamton 1985.

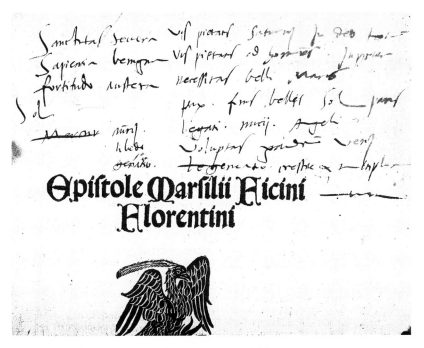

52 Marsilio Ficino, *Epistolae*, Venice 1495, Title-page.

and pagans demons. In their operations, they are rather different from the *demones* of Thomas More. The angels, says Ficino, strive to purify us even by dreams; the demons represent themselves to men as good, not evil, as gods to be worshipped. They sometimes operate by means of sensory effluences and flow into bodies. The demons of gluttony, for example, are attracted by meat and especially by hot, cooked meat. They enter it and make it demonic, so that they infect the man who gulps it down. They infect even the smell of food. So philosophers and theologians ought to beware of hot and steaming dishes, to keep out of restaurants and pagan temples alike, the scenes of secular and religious sacrifice. There is no doubt of the moral warning in Ficino's descriptions of these operations, but

tum patroni locum reliquerit ac ſtudio:Ꝓ-ſunc libru ad te dedimus iis qui curam
hic gerunt rerum illorum ex medicis:quo mittedo cum fidei & promiſſo noſtro
omnino tum ſtudiis tuis atque animo erga Platoné nō nihil ſatiſſactū eē putam?
bñ uale.&an librū accepis nos facies certiores ex urbe idibꝰſeptēbris.Mꜿꜿꜿlxix.
   De laude platonicorum interpretum.

  Marſilius Ficinus Florentinus Bexarion græco Cardiali Sabīo.S.D.

P Lato nr̄ uenerāde pr̄:cum i phedro ut te nō latet ſubtiliter ꝓ copioſe de
pulchritudie diſputaſſet pulchritudie aī a deo quā ſapiétiā:& aurū appel
lauit ꝓtioſiſſimū poſtulauit:aurū hoc platōi a deo tributū platonico i ſi
nu utpote mūdiſſimo fulgebat clariſſime . Verbis aūt & litteris licet luculentiſſi
mus meſite tamé obſcurioribus ſuolutū euaſit obſcurius:& quaſi terreno quodā
hābitu obſitū eos hoīes latuit:qui liceos oculos nō habebāt. Quamobré nōnul
li quondā minutiores philodoxi exteriori gleba decepti cū nō poſſet ad ītima pe
netrare latentē theſaurū cōtēnebāt:Verū ī Plotīm primū porphirii deinde & Iā
blici:ac deniꝗ ꝑculi officinā aurū illud ſniectū exquiſitiſſimo ignis exaīe ex cuſ
ſis arēis e nituit uſꝗ adeo ut omné orbé miro ſplédore replueuit.Tātis utiqꝫ ra
diis nóctue ſiue bubōes ꝗdā:ut uideẗ offēſi ſacrū illū Platonis nr̄i theſaurū nō ſo
lū ſpnere:ut nō nulli quondā:ſed ꝓoh nefas ſprobare cœperūt:qd multo erat pri
ori errore deterius. Verū Bexarion achademié lumen medelā cōſeſtim ebetibus
& caligatis oculis adhibuit ſaluberrimā:ut aurū illud nō ſolū mūdū ſit.& ſplendi
dū:uerū ēt tractābile manibus oculíſꝗ inoxiū.Hoc uaticinatus Plato fore tépus
multa poſt ſecula regi dyoniſio īquit quo theologiæ myſteria exactiſſima diſcuſ
ſiōe ueluti igne aurū purgarētur:Venerūt:ſā uenerūt ſecula illa Bexarion:quibus
& platonis gaudeat & numé & nos omnis eius familia ſūmope gratulemur. Vale.

   Exhortatio ad ſcientiam.

  Marſilius Ficinus Antonio pactio.S.D.

A Vretius medices:duoli te laudat præceteris magnificétiā & acumē:Lau
do & ego:ſed Antoni magnificétiẹ ꝗdé uſu cōpare tibi cẹteros potes:acu
minis aūt exercitatiōe cōpare tibi te ipſū:ſi tantū doctriæ ſtudueris quan
tū liberalitati ſandudū idulges nō dubito breui te ita omniū doctiſſimū fore quē
admodū nūc es magnificétiſſimus omniū.Age ꝓcor Antoni mi ſuauiſſime cōmé
da te ipſū tibi ſicuti cẹteros cōmédatos hēs.Lauretius nr̄ ait te nō mē erga doctos
magnificū eē uertū ēt abūde doctū.Credo eꝗdé atꝗ gratulor.At nō prius ſatis mi
hi feceris ꝗ tātū ſciétia ꝗtū magnanimitate excelleris:ſi tibi eruditiſſimi quiꝗ i
primis placét:da opā:ut tibi ipſe ꝓcæteris placeas:qd ergo ordo i oibus plurimū:
imo totū ualet:ſtatue oro tibi quotidie horas ꝗtuor̄reliquas: ut uſcꝗ placet:ami
cis dona.Bñ Vale:ſed uis ne ualere bñ:Benediſce:& diſce ꝓcor hodie. Qui cras
diſcit nunꝗ diſcit.yiii.Nouemb. Mꜿꜿꜿlxxiii. Conſolatio in alicuíus obitu.

  Marſilius Ficinus Siſmundo ſtuſe conſolationem dicit.

I ſꝗ nr̄um id maxie ē qd i nobis ē maximū qd pmanet ſemp idem:qua
nos ipſi capimus:certe aīus homo ipſe eſt corpus auté é hominis umbra

there is also a strong desire to be precise about just how these demons operate. One senses that the operation is less important for Colet than the moral.

In attempting to fulfil the obligations of my title, I have said something about some of the early Tudor humanists and some of their books. In doing so, I have tried to say something by implication about the nature of early Tudor humanism, and about its debt to Erasmus. With a natural mistrust of the general statement, I have tried chiefly to present specific items of evidence, to point out some of their implications, and to leave others to your interpretation. The men with whom I have been chiefly concerned are good company, and worth knowing more about. Every reading of them indicates not only how much there is still to be known, but how worthwhile is the effort to do so.

List of Items in the Exhibition
to accompany the Lectures:
King's Library, 9 November 1990 to 27 January 1991

LEARNING AND PIETY IN MANUSCRIPT AND PRINT

Pauline and Catholic Epistles in the Vulgate and Erasmian Versions
Royal MS 1 E. V, part ii, 1506–c.1530

John Colet's *Abbreviations* of Ps-Dionysius the Areopagite
Additional MS 63853, c. 1506

Book of Hours
Lambeth Palace Library MS 3561, c. 1516

William Tyndale's New Testament
C.23.a.8, 1534

The New Testament in Greek and Latin, edited and translated by
Desiderius Erasmus Roterodamus
C.24.f.14, 1516

Biblia Sacra, Hebraice, Chaldaice, Graece & Latine, edited by Benedictus
Arias Montanus
C.17.d.2, vol. ii, 1570

Thomas More, *Dissertatio epistolica, de aliquot sui temporis Theologas-
trorum ineptiis; Deque correctione translationis vulgatae N. Testamenti: Ad
Martinum Dorpium Theologum Lovaniensem*
3932.a.4, 1625

Thomas More, *Libellus vere aureus nec minus salvtaris quam festiuus de
optimo reip.statu, deque noua insula Vtopia* . . .
C.27.b.30, 1516

Desiderius Erasmus Roterodamus, *Moriae Encomium*
12316.f.37, 1512

Erasmus's copy of the *editio princeps* of Aristotle in Greek
King's College, Cambridge, XV.8.3, 1499

Marsilio Ficino, *Epistolae*
IB.22769, 1495

Giovanni Pico della Mirandola, *Heptaplus de septiformi sex dierum Gene-seos enarratione*
IB.27536, c1496

Galen, *De sanitate tuenda* and *Methodus medendi*, translated by Thomas Linacre
C.19.e.15, 17, 1517, 1519

Sir Thomas Elyot, *The Dictionary*
C.28.m.2, 1538

Johann Reuchlin, *De arte cabbalistica*
719.l.14, 1517

Giovanni Pico della Mirandola, *Exposition of Psalm XV* and *The twelve Weapons for Spiritual Battle*, in French
Royal MSS 16 E. XXIV and XXV, 1498

Girolamo Savonarola on Psalms L and XXX
Royal MS 16 E. XVI, early sixteenth century

Desiderius Erasmus, *Enchiridion militis christiani*
1010.b.7 (11), 1504

AN ENGLISH GRAMMAR SCHOOL EDUCATION

John Colet's Statutes for St Paul's School
Additional MS 6274, mid-sixteenth century

William Lily, *De generibus nominum, ac verborum praeteritis ac supinis regulae*
625.d.11, c. 1528

Desiderius Erasmus Roterodamus, *De duplici copia rerum et verborum*
1331.c.1 (2), 1512

DIALOGUE WITH BOOKS: ANNOTATIONS

St Augustine, *Opera omnia*
C.79.i.1 (vols. 7–8), 1532

Proba Falconia, *Carmina sive Centones Vergilii*
IA.12305, c1495

Augustinus Triumphus de Ancona, *Summa de potestate ecclesiastica*
IB.3131, 1475

The bokes of Salomon, namely: Proverbia. Ecclesiastices. Sapientia, and Ecclesiasticus, or Jesus the sonne of Syrach
C.25.b.4(1), 1542

Boethius, *De consolatione philosophiae*, with commentary
IA.47817, 1491

ADVICE FOR RULERS, MAGNATES AND PRIVATE PERSONS

Thomas More, Latin Verses on the Coronation of Henry VIII
Cotton MS Titus D.IV, 1509

Desiderius Erasmus Roterodamus, *Institutio principis Christiani*
526.k.2, 1516

Sir Thomas Elyot, *The Boke named the Gouernour*
C.40.b.36, 1531

Celso Maffei, *Tractatus ne principes ecclesiasticos usurpent census*
Additional MS 15673, c1505

Desiderius Erasmus, *A deuout treatise vpon the Pater noster*, translated by Margaret Roper
C.37.e.6(1), c1526

Diodorus Siculus, *Bibliotheca historica*
Arundel MS 93, 1482

Lucian of Samosata, *Three Dialogues*, in Latin, and Pandolfo Collenuccio, *Apologues*
Royal MS 12 C. VIII, c1509–17

Cuthbert Tunstal, *De arte supputandi*
C.54.d.4(1), 1522